# THE
# DELOREAN
# STORY

# THE
# DELOREAN
# STORY

## THE CAR, THE PEOPLE, THE SCANDAL

## NICK SUTTON

**Haynes Publishing**

*This book is dedicated to DMCL employee number 21, my wife Phyllis, who has been a constant daily reminder that many things in the DeLorean Dream were positive. And to my children, Christopher, Fiona and Nicole.*

© Nick Sutton 2013

First published in February 2013

A catalogue record for this book is available from the British Library

ISBN 978 0 85733 314 8

Library of Congress control card no 2012948591

Published by Haynes Publishing,
Sparkford, Yeovil, Somerset BA22 7JJ, UK
Tel: 01963 442030 Fax: 01963 440001
Int. tel: +44 1963 442030 Int. fax: +44 1963 440001
E-mail: sales@haynes.co.uk
Website: www.haynes.co.uk

Haynes North America Inc.,
861 Lawrence Drive, Newbury Park,
California 91320, USA

Printed and bound in the USA by Odcombe Press LP,
1299 Bridgestone Parkway, La Vergne, TN 37086

# CONTENTS

## Chapter 1

# HERO TO VILLAIN IN
# FOUR YEARS

'John DeLorean.' We shook hands.

My first meeting with John DeLorean in the reception area of the training building in Dunmurry was only a brief moment, but it's one that I shall always remember. A major refurbishment of the building, a former carpet warehouse, had just been completed to reflect the international status and grandeur of its new occupants: DeLorean Motor Cars Ltd. In this lobby just weeks earlier television crews, journalists and dignitaries had attended the groundbreaking ceremony to celebrate the foundation of the new enterprise.

The success of the venture was pivotal to the UK government's credibility in the investment policy they had planned for Northern Ireland. Jim Callaghan's Cabinet knew that the money provided to John DeLorean was a huge political and financial gamble. But as everything that had been tried in order to resolve the civil conflict that had raged through Northern Ireland for the previous ten years had so far failed, the investment in the DeLorean programme was thought to be well worth the risk. Over 700 deaths had been recorded in Northern Ireland during the previous four years, with a further 7,000 people injured, and all this despite the intervention of the 22,000 military personnel stationed in the province. The new car and modern factory were intended to bring jobs and confidence to Belfast. The government hoped that a successful operation would attract other overseas investors.

My short conversation with John DeLorean took place next to the full-size photograph of the DeLorean car (code name DMC12) adorning the wall of the reception stairwell. I was immediately impressed that a man known to everyone in the automotive business had felt the need to tell me his name; John DeLorean at his very best. The date was early December 1978.

During his visits to the factory at Dunmurry and Lotus he radiated a persona of confidence and certainty of purpose that permeated the two companies. His presence at Dunmurry, usually lasting no longer than a day, lifted the morale of those who had the opportunity to talk to the legend that was John DeLorean. They hoped he would make an irrevocable difference to their lives.

Three years later things had changed. The money was gone; the order book of 30,000 cars promised at the start of the programme had disappeared. The dream John DeLorean sold us had turned sour.

A year further on he was charged with drug offences. By this time the company was in receivership and the number of employees at Dunmurry had shrunk to a handful of people retained by the receiver to assist in the closure of the factory. I was one of the lucky few who stayed to the end.

Despite the trials, lawsuits and adverse publicity associated with his name, many in Belfast still regard

John DeLorean as the hero and the UK government the villain. John's endeavour to create jobs and improve the prosperity of the impoverished areas of Belfast remains his legacy. For many, there can be no debate regarding the sincerity of his mission.

Other ex-employees hold a different view, bitter that the man they had trusted failed them with his involvement in the drugs trade. His skirmish in drugs trafficking resulted in a trial in April 1984 in Los Angeles lasting four months before he was cleared of all charges in August of that year. Arrested in room 501 of the Sheraton La Reina hotel at Los Angeles airport on 19 October 1982 for holding $24 million of cocaine, he was charged with possession and various other drug offences. 'It's better than gold' were the words that condemned him in the eyes of the public.

The investigation by the FBI involved months of research, videotaping, and the recording of DeLorean employees' telephone calls in the USA and the United Kingdom.

On the day following his arrest we were told that the factory was to close at the end of the year. This was the end of the dream. No more government Seventh Cavalry charging over the Dunmurry Hills to save the financial remnants of the DeLorean wagon train, a scene we had experienced many times over previous years. It was closure for certain this time. This was the end.

John DeLorean's name was stained by his drugs trial, by missing equity money and allegations of misuse of public funds. These events tarnished the legacy of a talented man tempted by easy access to money provided by the British government; lax management allowed him to convert his dreams into cash and secure the lifestyle to which he had become accustomed.

The lifestyle stole the dream. The dream was now the lifestyle. The transition began in the President Wilson hotel in Geneva in late October 1978 when plans were made to skim off a significant amount of cash intended for the DeLorean car plant in Dunmurry. The commercial vehicle for the scam was GPD Services Inc., a shelf company in Panama used as a conduit to move money intended for the Belfast operation into other pockets. The GPD deal landed John DeLorean the biggest bonus of his seemingly charmed life.

For 30 years I'd not really given a thought to John DeLorean's vision, until I was persuaded to write this account and record the chronology of the company and its legacy. Many details I recall clearly, while other memories are jogged to life by reading journals of the time or my wife Phyllis filling in the gaps, as she was also an employee from the beginning of the venture.

This is the story of the DeLorean dream in Belfast and it details the events that resulted in its foundation and ultimate closure. It's a personal view, recording activities from the first visit of DeLorean personnel to Belfast in June 1978 and the groundbreaking ceremony in October 1978; through the car's development programme and short manufacturing period; the IRA hunger strikes and the production ramp-up to satisfy John DeLorean's public stock offering, which would make him a multi-millionaire; into receivership and the attempt to save the factory, foiled by Margaret Thatcher; and then closure of the factory in February 1983.

The story also offers one answer as to why Margaret

Thatcher rejected the recovery plans proposed by a UK consortium to restart production and to re-employ 1,100 ex-employees. The plan was backed by Sir Kenneth Cork, who had been appointed as the receiver for DeLorean Motor Cars Ltd, and the Secretary of State, James Prior. It was thwarted by the Prime Minister at a Cabinet meeting in August 1982, two months before John DeLorean's arrest on drug charges.

The car that carries John DeLorean's name lives on in the magnificent film *Back to the Future*, but it would be 20 years before I summoned the courage to watch the movie. Until then, I wouldn't allow my dream to be shared or stolen by anyone, whether film watcher, car owner or enthusiast. How could the popcorn audience understand the energy, determination, passion and sacrifice that had forged the car named DeLorean? These were my memories and not for sharing. I believed that the legacy of the little miracle in Dunmurry was mine alone. But the memories of the DeLorean experience also belong to 2,500 other ex-employees, of whom a judge said during one of the DeLorean trials: 'Many people employed at the company were ill prepared and ill equipped to cope with the gross misfortune when the DeLorean dream turned into a nightmare.'

The dream's first mistake occurred during negotiations with the UK government, when John DeLorean promised the first production cars in 18 months. He knew, as we did, that this was impossible, but he seduced the UK government with the promise of quick jobs before the impracticality of the timescale became apparent. The timing should have been questioned from the start; a more realistic date would have solved many problems. Instead, the challenge of achieving the impossible – to design and build a car factory in 18 months – was accepted both by the DeLorean employees and by Lotus.

The Dunmurry workforce was determined that this would be a success story in an environment where the only news was bad news. It was to be a mammoth challenge even if a year – a year we didn't have – was added to the timing.

As employee number 16 I worked with the senior management and directors of DeLorean from the beginning of the programme in 1978 to the end of the dream in January 1983, when only ten employees remained on the DeLorean Belfast site. A few weeks after I left the company the gates were padlocked and the liquidators moved in.

During my time with DeLorean I liaised with Lotus Cars in the development programme and attended the weekly development meetings at Lotus, Hethel in Norfolk. Two years after the collapse of DeLorean I joined the board of directors of Lotus Cars.

Revisiting the DeLorean dream after a third of a century has given a fresh perspective to my memories, my research revealing many aspects of the dream previously untold. Of course, every DeLorean employee will have a story to tell about their employment at the company, but this is mine.

For some involved in the dream, either viewing the drama from the sidelines or as an employee, this testimony may prove to be uncomfortable reading.

## Chapter 2

# LONDON AND BELFAST, 1978

The chamber was almost empty when the Speaker of the House of Commons called on Gerry Fitt, the member for West Belfast, to speak. It was the early afternoon of 26 May 1978; being a Friday and the eve of a short spring break, most MPs had taken the opportunity of an early start to their vacation. Fitt's speech was about Northern Ireland and most MPs showed as little interest in the affairs of that region as did the average person on the streets of London. Some people even hoped that the province would float away into the Atlantic and rid the United Kingdom of the gory mess that was Northern Ireland.

Gerry Fitt began by reminding the House that while Parliament was breaking for a short vacation many of his constituents were jobless and therefore on permanent holiday, without the prospect of returning to work. Radical action was required to resolve the problem of unemployment in his constituency. He passionately believed that the creation of jobs and the associated dignity of the pay packet would be the solution to the strife that plagued the province. Northern Ireland was in a state of civil war in all but name.

Fitt championed the cause of the oppressed and the unemployed, one of the few leaders from the Catholic community to publicly challenge the Provisional IRA about their regime of violence. He advocated peaceful rather than violent methods of political and social reform. During the 1970s he lobbied the UK government for assistance to reduce the obscene levels of unemployment in West Belfast and beyond. The terrorist organisations, particularly the IRA, found it easier to recruit support for their operations in areas of high unemployment.

Unemployment in Gerry Fitt's constituency averaged 30%, with higher levels in the Whiterock, Ballymurphy, Suffolk and Twinbrook housing estates. In these pockets of social deprivation the unemployment level reached 50%. UK state aid in the area, via social security payments, was the highest per capita in the United Kingdom and the wider European Community. There was little hope: many men in their thirties had never worked, and some families had three generations living in the same household who'd never had a job. Middle-aged men regarded by their civil servant assessors as unemployable were told by the local social security office not to bother to report each week, as others did, but simply sign the unemployment register to receive payments every three months. This instruction was the passive assignment of the poor to the scrapheap of life, the end of their hopes and dreams. That day, in May 1978, Gerry Fitt challenged the government to take action and invest money rather than troops in Belfast.

His speech was the catalyst that brought John

DeLorean to Northern Ireland and marked the first major attempt by politicians to change the face of Belfast for the better.

Roy Mason, Secretary of State for Northern Ireland, was sitting on the government benches in the House of Commons listening to Gerry Fitt's speech and he had taken note. He believed that justice for everyone – houses, jobs and hope – would be the solution to the Troubles that cursed the province.

'The Troubles' is a local Northern Irish phrase to describe the period between the late 1960s and the mid-1990s and the violent events, bombings and murders that occurred in Northern Ireland during that time. The Nationalists, mainly Catholic factions, demanded unification of Northern Ireland with the Republic of Ireland, while the Loyalist Protestant movements insisted Northern Ireland remain part of the United Kingdom. This was the conflict: two groups fighting for irreconcilable goals. When the DeLorean deal was completed the Troubles were halfway through their bloody cycle.

It is perhaps only the Irish who would describe this conflict as 'the Troubles', essentially a war in which more than 3,500 people were killed and a further 50,000 injured – and all within a population of only 1.6 million in an area no larger than the state of Connecticut. The word 'Troubles' diminishes the suffering and shame of the period. Most family circles in Northern Ireland had the misfortune to experience at least one of their number being badly injured or killed. I have 'trouble' with my car, my lawnmower or my roof, but 50,000 lives in Northern Ireland were permanently changed and families destroyed by individual tragedy during this time.

Industrialists were targeted for special treatment. Thomas Niedermayer, managing director of the Grundig factory in Dunmurry, a German national and honorary consul for West Germany in Northern Ireland, was kidnapped from his West Belfast home in late 1973 – this was the second attempt to abduct him within a week. James Nicholson, sales consultant for Strathearn Audio at Dunmurry, was murdered after leaving the Strathearn factory for Belfast airport in 1977. In February 1977 Jeffrey Agate, the managing director of the international chemicals giant DuPont, was shot and killed outside his home in Derry. In March 1981 Geoffrey Armstrong, director of employee relations for the car manufacturer British Leyland, was shot three times in the leg while in Dublin giving a speech to the Dublin Junior Chamber of Commerce.

Politicians fared no better. Airey Neave, the shadow Northern Ireland Secretary, died when his car was blown apart as he was leaving the House of Commons car park on 30 March 1979.

Many of these attacks were later ascribed to 'rogue elements' of the Republican movement – but rogue bullets and bombs still kill and that is of no consolation to the bereaved.

A few months before Gerry Fitt's speech, and before John DeLorean declared an interest in Northern Ireland, negotiations were in progress between the DeLorean team and the IDA (Irish Development Agency) in Dublin, along with Des O'Malley, the Minister for Commerce. The IDA offered an empty factory in

Limerick, in the Republic of Ireland, in which to build John DeLorean's dream car. The chosen site was once occupied by the Belgian company Ferenka – part of the AKZO Group – who at their peak had employed 1,400 staff. The bad news was that the managing director, Dr Tiede Herrema, had been kidnapped in October 1975 near his home in Limerick. He was eventually released by police three weeks later, following a siege at a house in             .

When John DeLorean learned of the offer from the IDA and the proposed location and its history he was far from impressed. Similarly, the IDA was concerned about DeLorean's grand ambitions to take over the global automotive industry. Consequently the Irish deal fell through.

The businessmen mentioned above represented companies from Holland, Germany, Belgium, England and the United States. Thousands of jobs were lost as a result of terrorist actions, with some companies withdrawing from Ireland. Per capita, Ireland in the 1970s was second in the global kidnapping table, only beaten by Sicily, which took first place for many years.

Chuck Bennington, the first managing director of the DeLorean factory in Belfast, said that John was concerned for his own safety and believed that harm would come to him in Northern Ireland in one way or another. John DeLorean made very few overnight stops in Belfast, and these only in the early days. Later in the programme he would return to London each evening. The criticism that he should have stayed for longer is unjustified – first, because the security threat was then perceived as real; and second, the team he employed were more than capable of performing their tasks without the daily intervention of their founder.

Daily life in Northern Ireland was difficult for everyone. Travelling through Belfast was often a nightmare, with army roadblocks at sensitive locations, demands for identification at each checkpoint and often a search of the vehicle. A search of body and belongings was mandatory when entering the main shopping area in Belfast city centre; access was exclusively through one of five pedestrian gates, making Belfast by default one of the world's first pedestrian-only shopping areas.

Firebombs were often smuggled through the army security posts so most stores undertook their own search of customers prior to them entering shop premises. Belfast became the only city where customers were searched entering stores rather than leaving.

Hoax bomb alerts often closed main traffic routes, meaning a short journey home could take several hours. This was before mobile phones, so an unplanned late arrival home of a loved one often gave cause for grave concern – as I was to learn some years later when a Catholic work colleague didn't make it home one night, or any night after that. He was murdered, a victim of hatred and sectarianism.

Bombs caused chaos and in one night alone, Bloody Friday, on 21 July 1972, 22 bombs exploded in Belfast. Shops, factory premises and hotels damaged by terrorist activity were rebuilt at the government's expense as private insurance didn't cover terrorist activity. The caveat was that owners had to reconstruct in the same location as the destroyed building to obtain compensation. Many did rebuild, but others didn't. Some who had paid protection money to the paramilitaries made their businesses unviable so the ruined buildings were left to decay. Burned-out buildings and derelict open spaces between high-rise blocks were evidence of a city in conflict.

Parking in sensitive areas was an issue. Notices were placed on the kerbside to identify parking regulations. A kerbside notice in a restricted area meant that at least one adult was required to remain in the vehicle otherwise the police would treat the vehicle as suspicious; the owner might return to find the vehicle in parts or the hood and trunk blown off by the security forces.

Hotels had their own idea of security. The Europa hotel in central Belfast had a large wooden hut erected close to the main road, outside the entrance. It was only possible to enter the hotel through this hut, which had a hand-painted sign on a large wooden plank nailed over the entrance marked 'Security' – and this was Belfast's premier hotel. In the search area of the hut, and with no privacy, the guests' belongings were investigated and thrown to the side as the security staff rifled through their baggage. A detailed hand-to-body frisk was thrown in for good measure. Then it was a short walk through the 'Exit' door in the hut to the hotel entrance.

Rioting became a national sport and occurred at the drop of a hat – usually at flashpoints where one religious community encountered another. In the early days of the Troubles ad hoc riots would ignite for the slightest reason, but the organisers quickly realised that without publicity their efforts were pointless.

To achieve maximum exposure, organisers would arrange for a riot to commence at a specific time and ensure that TV cameras were present. A television executive of the era recalls that on more than one occasion the TV newsroom would receive a message that a riot was to start at a certain location but not to be there until a certain time because it wouldn't begin until the allocated time. These clashes became controlled choreographed sessions, similar to sporting events, with an imaginary referee blowing the whistle for hostilities to begin. But there were no rules in this game. The toll of injury, destruction, misery and death were the only measures to assess the winning side.

The division between Protestant and Catholic communities was often only feet apart. Rioting and intimidation led to mass migration to a safer haven. The move could be just a few streets away, or the other side of town, or England, or even further afield. Parents encouraged their older children to emigrate in order to seek a better future, as their forefathers had done, further south in Ireland, a hundred years earlier during the great potato famine.

Twinbrook housing estate, close to the new DeLorean factory, was occupied in part by Catholic families fleeing from intimidation in Protestant areas in central Belfast. Many were so desperate for a home and sanctuary in their collective community that families squatted in partly built houses on the estate. Many houses were without doors or windows, the new occupants eager to ensure their right to tenancy before the buildings were allocated to others by the Belfast housing authorities.

Others went further afield. Brian Keenan, in his book

*An Evil Cradling*, describes his move from Belfast to the Middle East and drinking his last pint of Guinness in the Crown Bar opposite the Europa before going to the American University in Beirut. This move didn't work out well for him, however, as he was captured and held in solitary confinement for over four years by Islamic Jihad. Another migrant from Belfast, Neal Barclay (DeLorean clock number 1804), moved with his family from the leafy suburbs of East Belfast to the town of Antrim, in the process receiving government aid to assist with the moving costs.

Add all this trauma to the miserable weather in Northern Ireland and there was nothing pleasing to the eye or the soul in Belfast in the late 1970s. If it wasn't raining it had just stopped or was about to start. The outlook was always grim and the environment dark.

So welcome to Belfast in 1978 – Dodge City in all but name – complete with cowboys but little sign of the sheriff. He would arrive with the peace process 17 years later, on what the locals believed to be the slowest horse in town.

In late 1978, in a magnificent splash of Technicolor and glamour, John DeLorean came to Belfast, complete with his entourage. The scene could have been lifted from a Hollywood blockbuster, his glamorous wife Cristina the leading lady. The main player in the drama was, of course, the magnificent stainless steel gull wing sports car, then just a photograph and a couple of prototypes. Most important of all was the pocketful of money John DeLorean had been given by the UK government to spend in the area. This had not gone unnoticed by the locals; the British government had finally done something sensible.

Who could ask for more? The dream had landed. Everyone was going to work.

And for a wonderful few years, they did.

*Chapter 3*

# DMCL – A CREDIBLE ORGANISATION

To have credibility in Northern Ireland an acronym is essential. For example, the Royal Ulster Constabulary was the RUC, the Irish Republican Army was the IRA, and the Northern Ireland Development Agency was NIDA. Then there are the political parties, including the DUP (Democratic Unionist Party), the UUP, PUP, SDLP and the newly formed TUV – and if you confuse the paramilitary UVF with the LVF or the UFF you'll only do this once. And just when these acronyms begin to make sense they're changed. The RUC became the PSNI, the IRA is now PIRA and NIDA now INI.

It's from this background that the DeLorean factory in Belfast became DMCL.

Just 23 days after Gerry Fitt's passionate plea in the House of Commons the first DeLorean representatives arrived in Northern Ireland, flying from London to Aldergrove airport, located 20 miles north of Belfast city, on Sunday 18 June 1978. They may have been uncomfortable with the intense security in and around Aldergrove, but once past the army checkpoint station a mile from the airport, things began to look normal. They relaxed. Ireland, as every American imagines, is home to rich, lush, green grass, a pleasant rural landscape, mountains in the distance, the occasional lake… Maureen O'Hara sitting in a donkey cart singing an Irish shanty would have completed the scene.

The journey to the Europa hotel in the centre of Belfast took the new M2 motorway, linking the north-east of Northern Ireland with Belfast. As the representatives approached Belfast the scenery changed. Over a hill, three miles from the city, appeared one of the most recognisable scenes of an industrial heartland to be found in Europe: Belfast Lough, glistening in the summer sunshine a hundred feet below as it narrowed towards the city to become the River Lagan. The twin super-cranes of Harland and Wolff dominate the landscape. These two immense structures, named 'Sampson' and 'Goliath', impose their yellow 100m-high structures over the dockyard. The backdrop to the scene, the green hills of North Down, sweep down to Belfast Lough, kissing the shoreline at the harbour entrance.

A little further and Belfast city appeared; a mile onwards and the scenery changed again. Tight security, an army roadblock or a burned-out building bore witness to a city in the grips of civil war. The taxi stopped outside the Europa, on the main road close to the security hut entrance, and after a baggage check they went through the small, temporary wooden extension that was doubling as a bomb-blast door, to the main entrance and into the hotel foyer and lobby.

Not much was happening in Belfast that Sunday in 1978. No shops were open; all the bars and pubs were closed. Given the security situation they'd have thought it unwise to walk around the city centre, although in Belfast in June natural light can remain until 11pm. The television news wouldn't have given them much comfort. The local headlines told the story of a Catholic priest, Father Murphy, taken hostage as barter for the release of an RUC officer kidnapped the previous day.

The following day John DeLorean joined the Europa team, choosing to fly in that morning rather than stay overnight in Belfast. Their first meeting with NIDA took place at their headquarters in Holywood, three miles from Belfast centre. NIDA's offices were then adjacent to Palace Army Barracks and were therefore well protected.

In the evening the team returned to the Europa hotel. As they turned to that friend of every traveller, the television, the local news bulletin recorded Margaret Thatcher's visit to Belfast earlier in the day. Her Conservative party were then in opposition but well ahead in the polls. If the predictions were correct Prime Minister Jim Callaghan and the Labour party would soon be out of office and the new crew led by Margaret Thatcher would be installed as the ruling party of the United Kingdom – which includes Northern Ireland.

By 21 June a draft deal had been signed between DeLorean and the government. On 26 June the DeLorean team returned to Belfast. Shaun Harte, a new recruit to NIDA, was introduced into the negotiations. Shaun was later to become a board member of DMCL; a man I got to know well.

During the last week of June Shaun Harte, with George Wilson from NIDA, Frank McCann from the Department of Commerce and Robin Bailie, a local Belfast solicitor, travelled to the DeLorean offices in the

US to undertake due diligence, to assess the viability of the car programme and to judge the risk of the UK government's potential investment. On their return they gave a positive response to Ronnie Henderson, the chief executive of NIDA.

Approval for public funds for the DeLorean project was given at Jim Callaghan's Cabinet meeting on 26 July 1978. The Northern Ireland Secretary of State, Roy Mason, argued that the government should vote in favour of the investment, stating that 'Catholic West Belfast has critically high male unemployment and is in real danger of degenerating into a ghetto. The best way to counter the influence of the IRA in the area is to provide new jobs. It is therefore of the utmost political, social and psychological importance that the project should go ahead.' The Cabinet agreed to the investment.

On 28 July the parties signed the master agreement – a 20-page document setting out the responsibilities and obligations of each party. In one paragraph the contract defined Belfast as 'convenient to suitable labour catchment areas', an understatement of epic proportions. The document also noted that John DeLorean's contract of employment allowed him a salary of $298,750 a year. His other interests were recorded as a director of Chris-Craft, the boat maker in the US.

On 2 August a press announcement put out by Roy Mason explained the deal. He told the nation that DeLorean Motor Cars Ltd already had 30,000 orders for the car in the US; a dealer network was also in place. As I listened to Roy Mason's speech at home that evening in England I wondered how I could become involved in the programme. Starting with a greenfield site and a clean sheet of paper sounded attractive to anyone with ambition.

The initial investment by the UK government amounted to £53 million; the master agreement included a royalty payment to the government of $375 per car for the first 90,000 vehicles. The DeLorean Research Limited Partnership, a group of 140 investors in the US, owned the design rights of the car and would be eligible for a royalty payment of the same amount, while loans guaranteed by the government would be converted to grants providing the expected employment levels were achieved.

The site chosen in mid-August comprised 72 acres on the outskirts of Dunmurry. This was an ideal location for a car plant, given the high level of unemployment in the area. There were two streams to divert or culvert, hence the name Twinbrook for the housing estate adjacent to the site. Twinbrook is a Catholic housing estate with the church of St Luke's half a mile from the entrance to the new site. At the other end of the fields is Seymour Hill, a Protestant housing estate which had two tenement blocks that gave full view of the new site and the Twinbrook housing estate half a mile away. On the edge of the site near to Twinbrook was 50,000 square feet of ex-carpet warehouse, with office accommodation on two floors. For some DeLorean staff this became home for the next four years.

A groundbreaking ceremony took place on 2 October 1978 in and around this building. Earlier, the first DMCL board meeting confirmed the foundation of the company: John DeLorean, Bill Collins, Dick Brown and Myron Stylianides were among those who attended the short meeting in the improvised boardroom.

Don Concannon represented Roy Mason, Secretary of State for Northern Ireland, at the ceremony. Other attendees included Gerry Fitt, the local Member of Parliament for West Belfast, and the Lord Mayor of Belfast. From the DeLorean US team Jerry Williamson, Dixon Hollinshead and his wife Barbara (known as BJ) were added to the list of guests. The religious front was covered by Canon Pádraig Murphy, a man of immense stature both pastorally and physically.

The assembled visitors, reporters and TV crew moved outside to a small marquee, erected to shelter the visitors from the ubiquitous rain that plagues Northern Ireland, and to offer a degree of protection and privacy for the dignitaries to plant three trees to commemorate the occasion. A copper plaque recording the details of the ceremony was mounted on a concrete base laid in the grass near to the perimeter fence.

Demonstrators protesting about IRA prisoner conditions in the H block of the Maze prison gathered on the other side of the wire fence only a few feet away and spoilt the scene. The protesters were keen to catch the world's eye as they knew the event was being attended by the US press. This was too good an opportunity to miss.

The party moved back indoors and into the training building where some guests gave speeches. A champagne toast in the reception area adjacent to the stairwell and a photo shoot with the political dignitaries rounded off the proceedings.

This stairwell was to witness many significant events

over the years: the good and the famous treading the steps to make their way to the boardroom; meeting my future wife, Phyllis, for the first time as we crossed on the stairs in January 1979; soldiers squatting on the halfway landing adorned with facial blackout, body armour, SLR rifles and riot gear. This last scene occurred two-and-a-half years further into the programme, but for now it was a time of celebration.

Twenty-eight-year-old Cristina Ferrare stole the show in a beige tweed suit and knee-high boots. She was asked by a local reporter if she minded if her boots had lost their shine in the mud during the tree-planting ceremony. She laughed, dismissed the comment and continued to follow her husband. Then the bulldozers started work. JMJ Contractors of Banbridge were tasked with the job of clearing the fields to allow Dixon Hollinshead and his crew to commence the real work the next day. Local children crowded around the huge bulldozers, dwarfed by the earthmovers' huge tyres.

Dixon Hollinshead had been invited to Belfast by Dick Brown to undertake the conversion of the ex-carpet warehouse into offices and headquarters for the first phase of the programme. It was only when he was introduced to the NIDA team a few weeks later that he learned that he was to take charge of building the complete site. This was surprising news, as he'd intended to stay for only a short time to refurbish just one building. Dick Brown had previously used Dixon's expertise to build the Mazda facilities in the US. Hollinshead, a towering man, made things happen. He was not the argumentative type: you did exactly as he asked or you didn't do it at all. Dixon was one of five key people who eventually made the DeLorean operation happen. Without his drive and will to overcome the many and various obstacles there would not have been a DeLorean factory.

As the surveyors, builders and architects were making their plans, John DeLorean was looking at the bigger picture. His objective was to find a company to engineer and design his car. He had already researched various options, including Porsche, who quoted seven years and £40 million; for BMW, it was four years and £50 million.

John turned to Lotus Cars, located in Norfolk, in the east of England and 400 miles from Belfast across the Irish Sea. In July he arrived at Lotus for his first visit, travelling to the factory from Heathrow by helicopter. After prolonged negotiations the deal with Lotus was completed in late October 1978.

His next decision was to confirm Renault as a supplier for the drive train. John DeLorean had held discussions with the French company for several years. He signed a draft contract in February 1978, ready to be executed once the manufacturing plans and locations were in place. The engine, a 2.8-litre V6 unit, was manufactured at the PRV facility in Douvrin, northern France. The engine had originally been designed by Peugeot, Renault and Volvo (PRV) to meet Federal EPA (Environmental Protection Agency) requirements and was thought to be a good choice for DeLorean's dream machine. The proximity of the engine manufacturing plant and the commercial terms were almost perfect. Credit of 120 days would assist cash flow and the unit cost of £1,200 for the engine and transaxle was certainly competitive.

Someone to design the plant with knowledge of automotive assembly would be the next step. That task was awarded to the industrial arm of Renault: Société d'Etudes et de Réalisation Industrielle, more commonly and very fortunately known by their acronym SERI. Henri Levy became their resident engineer at Dunmurry.

During this period Chrysler, now led by Lee Iacocca, were withdrawing from their European operations as dictated by the US government under the terms of their financial support for the company. The personnel director of Chrysler Europe, Myron Stylianides, was offered a position on the main board of DMCL. He resigned from Chrysler and commenced work at the DeLorean factory immediately. It was Myron who wrote my offer of employment on 31 October 1978, just a few weeks after he started work at Dunmurry.

Chuck Bennington was hired as managing director and president of DMCL. He'd been senior assistant to the president of Chrysler in Europe. Chuck had enormous experience in building plants throughout Europe and Asia and had been known to Myron for some time. The process went on from there, with more Chrysler people being employed at the beginning and again much later in the programme. These inevitably became known as the 'Chrysler Mafia'. The group was to supply interesting information throughout the programme, relayed from ex-colleagues who remained employed by Chrysler in the US.

The jigsaw was complete. It had been a long haul for John DeLorean. In 1975 he had given the task of styling his car to he had someone to design and develop the car, Lotus; to supply the power unit, Renault; to design the plant, SERI; and staff of a calibre more than capable of putting all the parts in place. There was government funding of £53 million, £7 million from the European Community and, to make the whole thing viable, 30,000 cars already sold as announced by the Secretary of State, Roy Mason, in August. What a start!

Yes, a credible organisation, DMCL.

*Chapter 4*

# MEET THE FAMILY

In October 1978 Barrie Wills accepted the position of purchasing director at DMCL. A man of short fuse and aggressive nature, to be sure, but if John DeLorean needed anyone to get things done it would be Barrie. Patience was not on his list of virtues. For some, his dismissive attitude towards non-performers could be less than diplomatic. I learned to tolerate his aggression and the firework displays that made a Saturn rocket look timid. I enjoyed his company, although approaching him was like relighting a firecracker that had failed to explode: you never knew if you would be losing a body part when you got close to the action, or if it would be a non-event.

Barrie asked if I would be interested in joining DMCL. It was a question he didn't need to ask twice.

A few weeks later, in mid-October 1978, I arrived at Aldergrove airport on my first visit to Northern Ireland. Waiting in the arrivals hall was Bobby, the company driver, ready to take me to Dunmurry. After a brief conversation I was convinced that I'd landed in a foreign country because I didn't understand a word he said. This was a two-way view because he didn't understand anything I said either.

The trip to Dunmurry was grim: army checkpoints here and there; the rubble of burned-out buildings; kerbstones painted in the colours of the local community's flag of choice. It was all very disturbing. Bobby, now speaking with a deliberate slowness to ensure I clearly understood, gave me a history of the Troubles condensed to 30 minutes of travelling time. He spoke with the enthusiasm of a London tourist guide highlighting the majestic buildings of the capital city, although he was actually explaining the scars of the landscape as we passed any building that had experienced recent trauma. This building was bombed when... followed by a description of the circumstances of the localised conflict. His repartee continued for building after building, street after street. Bobby certainly knew his local history and geography – and how to terrify newcomers.

I was looking forward to arriving at the factory. The building would surely offer some comfort and safety. The reality was different from the picture I had painted in my mind minutes earlier. Entering the Twinbrook gate to the factory I was relieved to see that the training building, where I was to be based, was surrounded by a high wire fence. But as we approached the structure I could see that although the fence was designed to keep out the boldest of cattle it would do nothing to deter any terrorist aged six years or older from entering the grounds.

Eamonn Rice, the managing director's security adviser and driver, greeted me at the entrance. He gave rudimentary advice about my personal safety and appeared to enjoy the sheer terror on my face when he said 'keep away from the windows', a warning he relished repeating throughout the day.

Having accepted the job, I returned on 4 December 1978 as employee number 16. Barrie introduced me to Chuck Bennington, managing director of DMCL. Meeting Chuck for the first time was a significant culture shock. He was wearing a black turtleneck top, jeans and cowboy boots. In other automotive companies where I had worked senior managers wore business suits complete with appropriate neckties. As I held out my hand to shake his I was expecting him to say 'howdy', like the characters in John Wayne films. But Chuck's clothes hid a formidable personality and an immense ambition to succeed. I suppose it was at this stage I guessed that DMCL wasn't going to be a normal place to work.

I was offered the choice of many vacant offices on the first floor of the training building, which overlooked the construction site. The building was all but empty; a scene I'd not witness again for another four years. I settled in and unloaded my meagre possessions, planning to obtain my stationery requirements from the stock cupboard. No luck – there wasn't one. This really was the start.

There were few amenities, apart from a coffee room on the first floor. One bonus was that the receptionist sitting at the base of the stairwell was terrifically attractive; she was a former beauty queen. This humble building was to be transformed from a former carpet warehouse to host a glamorous international company, becoming the centre of attention of the world's press, but so far there was only a beauty queen and several large photographs of the DeLorean car.

I was introduced to John DeLorean, who was in Dunmurry for a brief visit. He put out his hand, said 'John DeLorean', and shortly afterwards caught the plane to London and travelled on to Lotus in Norfolk. I met some of Bill Collins's team in the coffee room later that day. Marshall Zaun, ebullient and full of confidence, was there to assist in the factory's construction. It struck me immediately that he was dressed informally too; he was wearing chequered golf trousers and a casual shirt without a tie. Had he just arrived off a long-haul flight and not had time to change? I began to wonder if I'd led a sheltered life up until now. This must be how the international jet set were dressing these days.

The coffee room and rest area were to the rear of the building on the first floor. On one visit, and eager to get on with things, I walked back to my office, coffee in hand, passing Buck Penrose's office on the way. Buck was vice president of corporate planning and a right-hand man of John DeLorean. I couldn't fail to notice a huge chalkboard on the longest wall of his office, like those used in school years ago. There, in several colours, was the biggest and grandest critical path analysis I have seen from that day to this. There were several hundred event squares and decision markings. The length of this grand design was 12ft and it was 4ft high.

Buck took me through the process. On the left of the board, at the start, a multitude of arrows indicated input, while 12ft later a small dot with a milliard of lines pointing to a circle indicated the first production vehicle. How impressive was that, a plan in such detail, and the company had only been going for a few weeks.

Buck Penrose had good intentions in drawing such a grand plan, but the reality was that we had nothing yet, just a photograph of the Bill Collins prototype car – which looked magnificent – with some costs put together by DeLorean US staff for NIDA and that was it. This wasn't just the ground floor of a plan, it was the basement. There had been no production or design work undertaken on the car's design; at least not on the car we were to build.

My first task was to assess the material cost of the car and estimate the capital expenditure required for production tooling. I was given a large photograph of the Bill Collins prototype (that particular car was eventually to become known as Doris 1a). As the basic bill of materials I used the Renault power train, the VARI (Vacuum Assisted Resin Inject) process for the underbody and a stainless steel skin for the outer panels. I had costed vehicles before, but usually I had been provided with a parts list or a product profile, and certainly something more than a photograph. I asked for more information on the car, as I couldn't go further without more detail.

'Could I see the Bill Collins prototype?' I asked. The answer was 'No'. I was told that was all the information I was going to get at this stage, as the car hadn't yet been designed. The next day I was given a 1:30 scale plastic kit model of a Lotus Esprit, with the suggestion that I build the kit up from the chassis and cost the parts as I put them together.

I commenced my task of assembling the plastic kit car with the enthusiasm of a child and immediately began to enjoy this new job. My nose buried in the instruction manual, glue everywhere, my tongue halfway out to one side of my mouth, deep in thought, I was soon making good progress. It was like being in another world – or back to my childhood. Then I heard the voice of John DeLorean in the next office, on the telephone to his maid in the US and enquiring about the health of his children. What if he came into my office and saw his latest high-flying executive assembling a plastic kit car? My incomplete masterpiece was relegated to the desk drawer and eventually to a cupboard at home, where it lies to this day. I didn't use the model again.

A few days later I was given a parts book for the Lotus Esprit and I costed the DMC12 from this and from Chuck's verbal description of the vehicle interior. The Esprit parts book might have looked far more professional on my desk, but it was less fun than the plastic kit car.

I returned each week until Christmas 1978, completing work on the material costs and capital investment requirements for the car. Both appeared to be increasing in cost by the day. As I had learned, extra unit cost results in additional weight which in turn leads to lower miles per gallon – a vicious circle. This foreshadowed a problem we were to face just prior to production in late 1980 with the EPA.

As there were only a handful of us on site at this stage I got to know about most things that were happening. I heard in the coffee room that John was planning to buy Lotus Cars, a fact that thrilled some. I was less enthusiastic. Why buy a small company when you've got all the money to start from scratch and develop your own? The idea didn't make sense.

However, someone forgot to tell Colin Chapman that his company was for sale so that deal fell through.

Lengthy negotiations in Geneva then followed, involving Chapman, Fred Bushell and John DeLorean, and a deal was struck for Lotus to develop the car on a contract basis.

Lotus Cars agreed to engineer the car, but only on Colin Chapman's terms, in that the contract had to be arranged in the most tax-efficient manner possible. A press release issued on 15 November 1978 announced that Lotus would co-operate in the completion of the design and development of the DeLorean car.

By March 1979 I had met most of the new team. Chuck Bennington, DMCL's first managing director and an ex-Chrysler employee, as mentioned earlier, was a man of immense drive and ambition. Providing you were selected as a colleague and did exactly as you were asked things would be fine. Chuck had his enemies and could be brash to those around him that weren't part of his team. Fortunately, I was in his circle.

Joe Daly, also from Chrysler, became finance director and sat on the main board of directors. Joe was not the easiest of people to get along with, his roar declaring that he was the alpha male in the building – tackle him at your peril. Most of his staff were also ex-Chrysler.

Bob Donnell was appointed production control and traffic director. Also ex-Chrysler, Bob was a quiet man who clearly had ability; he employed many talented individuals who played key parts in the DMCL story. Martin Graham, then in his late twenties, was in charge of materials and he was the most gifted manager I have ever met. He later rose to fame in the US as vice president of a US national railroad company. Harry Steadman, ex-General Motors UK, whose forte was moving the unmoveable, had the added ability of walking through brick walls while not being sure what was on the other side when he performed this trick. This second line of management, to which I belonged, played a significant part in the building of the company; we were all between 28 and 34 years of age.

Mike Loasby joined the company as product engineering director. Mike was formerly managing director of Aston Martin Engineering Ltd. He was employed under misleading circumstances, as he mentioned in the BBC documentary *Car Crash*, in that he was contracted to convert a prototype car into a production car. This wasn't, in fact, the case, because the design of the DeLorean car started from scratch at Lotus in January 1979.

George Broomfield, manufacturing director, came from General Motors and had significant knowledge of car assembly operations. Although only ten years older than Barrie and Mike, he was regarded as the father figure in the group. George enjoyed an even temperament and was approachable. He rarely became angry, but a look of disdain from George could wither the strongest of individuals. George was liked and respected by everyone who worked with him; he often acted as a mediator between the rival factions of DMCL when they disagreed over the direction of the development programme.

Dick Mullholland became manager of the body shop,

the toughest job in the company. It suited the most able man manager in Dunmurry.

Shaun Harte had been working on the DeLorean programme full-time from the start of the programme in June 1978, but as a director on the main board and employed by NIDA. He eventually joined the company full-time on 1 December 1979. He had been a key figure in putting together the original deal between DeLorean and the government. Later in the programme he was nominated as the director in charge of the development programme. His job was to report progress of the venture to the main board; in doing so he became the company's referee and chief diplomat. During the frequent disagreements between directors over policy and direction Shaun acted as the referee, often retiring from scraps with more bruises than the fighters.

On his arrival Shaun was given my office. I was evicted to a temporary location and was eventually given a room under the stairs at the rear of the training building. My new location was a room without windows and natural light, and was to become known as the 'broom cupboard', a title that requires no further description.

Gene Cafiero joined the main board as president after leaving the same position at Chrysler, where he'd been replaced by Lee Iacocca. Gene appeared on the scene some time in early 1979, starting on an annual salary of $375,000 and also enjoying a one-off payment of $164,000 as compensation for loss of his bonus provisions at Chrysler.

Most of the second-line management were given the carrot and stick treatment by Gene, with a verbal bashing and a dash of humiliation at the end. Somehow he always seemed to have left the carrot at home on the days he'd pick a victim. At times he appeared lost in the morass of issues requiring resolution. His relationship with John DeLorean deteriorated as time progressed. Midway in his term of office it became obvious to everyone that the two were not on good terms, at times not even speaking.

In November 1980 Don Lander replaced Chuck Bennington as managing director; Don had been managing director of Chrysler's English operations, located in Coventry. Six months later George Lacey (who was appointed managing director for Chrysler UK after Don Lander) joined the Dunmurry team as engineering director. This was to allow Mike Loasby time to design and develop the four-seater DeLorean sedan car (the DMC24).

The two government representatives on the main board of directors were Alex Featherson (a licensed solicitor and member of the Northern Ireland Advisory Committee of the Department of Commerce) and James Sim, one-time general manager of the Bank of Ireland.

Bruce McWilliams appeared in April 1981, at first assisting Dick Brown in the US with the sales and marketing, then replacing Dick a few weeks into receivership in 1982. One of Bruce's former employers was British Leyland in the US; by coincidence, I'd had dealings with Bruce many years earlier when I worked as the personal assistant for the supplies director of Rover–Triumph in Coventry.

Ronnie Henderson, chairman of NIDA, was on the board for a few months. He was replaced by Tony Hopkins, who took over the job when Ronnie retired.

DeLorean employed some of the most talented managers in the automotive business, but many arrived with three pieces of baggage which would ultimately not help the project. The first was the kind of ego that is often found in successful people; the second was a previous company's procedure manual; and the third was a preconception of how to run a car company and develop a new product – which, by industry standards of the time, was taking five years or more.

We had 18 months to build a factory, train a workforce and produce a car. To achieve this goal, effective leadership was essential and the senior people had to be united. However, the directors squabbled from the beginning of the programme. This was evident to all of us at the next management level, the flak permeating down through the company. Some directors thought that the car should be designed and released in the orthodox manner and so take longer than the 18 months that we'd been given, while others thought differently.

But timing and planning were not the only issues we faced. Excessive overheads, particularly the cost of non-productive staff, were another problem. They would eat away at our working capital and remain unchallenged throughout the short life of the company.

Myron Stylianides had designed the management structure, but many of us who had worked for smaller companies, where staff levels and associated overheads were one of the keystones of a profitable operation, questioned the need for many of the management positions that were being advertised. Myron had taken the organisational chart from Chrysler, filled in the boxes of a skeleton structure and appointed people to fill in the blanks, regardless of need. Inevitably, we became top-heavy in the areas of finance and administration. Eventually we were to have 286 supervisory and management staff. Even a compensations manager adorned the organisation chart. (In my next life, if law school is full, I'll be taking a job as a compensations manager; I never learned what one does but it sounds very interesting.)

I wondered how I would perform among these great names, and hoped that I would be up to the challenges that lay ahead. But there would be times when I would doubt my own tenacity and ability.

*Chapter 5*

# LOTUS CARS AND THE USAAF AT HETHEL

The four Pratt & Whitney engines roared to their maximum 2,700rpm to lift the 56-ton B24 Liberator bomber into the sky above Hethel airfield. As the plane gained height, the pilot could see the outline of the station's priest at the end of the runway, waving and blessing each plane as it took off for its usual targets in Germany and beyond. The blessing of warriors departing for the battlefield was a Christian tradition that went back a thousand or more years. Earlier, the celebrant had given absolution and Holy Communion to the Catholic crew members. The priest, Father Gerald Beck, a Franciscan friar, provided pastoral care for his flock of 2,900 airmen and support staff at Hethel airfield. The year was 1944.

The Liberator was one of 48 planes, split into four squadrons, at Hethel. They belonged to the 389th Heavy Bomb Group. Father Gerald Beck's pastoral life was tucked away in his chapel at the rear of Hethel Woods, 300 yards from the main administration buildings. On the inner gable end of the improvised chapel a scene of the crucifix had been painted by one of the Hethel airmen. The mural remains intact to this day.

We were travelling at 150mph towards the end of

the runway. I thought that the 'pilot' might give some thought to slowing down. He didn't. This was the end. We were gone. John Miles was driving a Ferrari 308GTB around the Lotus test track. The car was owned by DMCL and I was in the passenger seat. It was February 1979. Hethel was now home to Lotus Cars.

At the end of the former runway was a sharp bend that an experienced driver would take at a maximum of 50mph. John drove the car through that corner at 120mph. I was convinced that I was losing my sight, with the G-force shifting my brain a little bit to the left. He asked if I'd like to go around the track again, but I declined. I wanted to retain some semblance of composure and dignity on my exit from the car.

What I couldn't know then was that I was to take the tour around the Lotus test track many more times over the next ten years and eventually drive the circuit behind the wheel of a Lotus product, albeit at a more leisurely pace and as a director of Lotus Cars.

John Miles was a gifted driver. He had raced Formula 1 cars for Colin Chapman at Team Lotus, competing with legends like Jochen Rindt, Graham Hill and others. John was now employed as a development driver for Lotus, one of the saner men in an environment where Colin Chapman nurtured drivers and engineers to view problems differently. John was an oasis of reason and had a maturity of vision that I treasured on each occasion he drove me round the Lotus circuit; he would explain that this suspension bush or another required a change to its hardness to enable the car to corner or handle better. He was not only a qualified engineer but also had significant experience in driving and assessing high-performance cars.

Hethel was assigned USAAF airfield number 114 in 1943. Later in the war, Hethel became home to the 389th Heavy Bombardment Group led by William Ellsworth Kepner, lieutenant general of the 2 Bombardment Division. From July 1944 James 'Jimmy' Stewart, the Hollywood actor, then a lieutenant colonel, became the general's assistant at the Hethel base.

George Wimpey Ltd began the construction of the airfield in August 1942. (Wimpey are now more commonly known as domestic house builders.) It was from this airfield and the accompanying buildings, including one of the former USAAF hangars, that the DeLorean car was tested and developed by Lotus between January 1979 and December 1980.

Colin Chapman founded Lotus Cars in 1947. His first factory, in Hornsey, north London, was little more than a group of garages either side of a railway track. One former employee, Albert Adams, recalls that a visit to the washroom entailed looking both ways up and down the track before crossing it to get to the necessary building. In 1959 Lotus moved to Cheshunt, a few miles north of London. With the success of the Lotus 7, a simple, lightweight, two-seater open-top sports car, the company expanded rapidly and urgently required a new location for manufacturing and testing vehicles. Ideally this was to be in a rural area as the current location, in the centre of a small town, had given rise to complaints about the noise, particularly at unsociable hours.

Such locations were available in Norfolk, a

hundred or so miles north-east of London. The area boasted a considerable number of ex-USAAF airfields and one of these, a few miles east of Norwich, was the Hethel airfield.

Lotus moved to Norfolk with its key people in 1966. When Lotus took over the airfield groups of buildings on the complex were allocated numbers as designations of location. One of these was the administration building constructed in 1940 and used by the USAAF for planning and intelligence; it was now designated as Factory 6 by Lotus. Jimmy Stewart, Jimmy Doolittle and the brave Americans from the 389th Heavy Bomb Group had trodden the floor of this same building 35 years earlier. This small complex was later to house the design team for the DeLorean project.

The USAAF runway was shortened by Lotus and used as a test track and landing strip for Colin Chapman's three aeroplanes, two twin-engined Cessnas and a Citation executive jet. On the edge of the test track was a new small hangar complex for these planes. Outside, adjacent to this building, was a landing pad for Colin's Bell Ranger helicopter. (Tony Rudd, engineering director at Lotus, called the fleet 'Lotus Airways'.) From here, visitors arriving by air could walk to the Lotus offices or, more usually, the company limousine would drive them the short distance.

The original control tower used by the USAAF, located mid-test track, had several purposes for Lotus. The ground floor became a training school, another room housed a museum for the USAAF, while the top floor became the Lotus social club.

The Lotus factory complex is built 180 degrees to the

traditional layout. The office complex and reception area, with gardens complete with fountains, enjoyed the best view, facing towards the airfield. The rear of the factory, displaying all its industrial glory, the car parks and material stillage storage bins, overlooked the road entrance. The idea was that as Colin Chapman generally brought his visitors and customers to Hethel by plane or helicopter they would see his factory from its best aspect – and it worked. First impressions count. The front view of the factory looks magnificent. No car factory in the world looked like that in 1978.

Under the 'Moonraker' name, Lotus manufactured large pleasure boats. It was for these structures that Lotus developed the VARI process, later to be used by Lotus Cars and DeLorean. VARI was developed over the years by Albert Adams; the plastics guru at Lotus was then the longest-serving employee of the company and perhaps one of the most memorable. VARI was introduced to replace the traditional labour-intensive hand-lay method of glass fibre production for large structures.

Chris-Craft, the US boat maker, entered the scene in 1977, developing a relationship with Lotus to market the Lotus Moonraker product line in the US and using the VARI process under licence for Chris-Craft products made in the USA. Colin Chapman and Tony Rudd visited the chairman of Chris-Craft, Herbie Siegel, at his offices in New York on numerous occasions to discuss design issues and commercial arrangements for the VARI process and the Moonraker product range.

By the grace of his old friend Herbie Siegel, whom he'd met socially while working at General Motors,

John DeLorean had temporary offices at Chris-Craft on Madison Avenue; he was also a director of the company. Colin Chapman and Tony Rudd met John DeLorean there for the first time in early 1977.

Shortly after this first meeting, Tony Rudd was approached by John DeLorean to become engineering director for his new car company. The job would be based in Detroit. Following prolonged discussions, and a visit to the USA by Tony and his wife, he declined the offer. In his book *It Was Fun!* Tony explains the episode in detail and describes how it affected his relationship with Colin Chapman. Colin clearly knew of the ongoing discussions between him and John DeLorean but rarely mentioned it in conversation.

When John DeLorean made his first visit to Hethel, in July 1978, Mario Andretti was the lead driver for Team Lotus. He became Formula 1 World Champion that year, with Lotus winning the Constructors' Championship, to the delight of Colin Chapman. John DeLorean wanted the fingerprints of Lotus Cars all over his car, as did others a few years later when Lotus Engineering became a roaring success.

That first visit by John DeLorean to Lotus included a trip to Group Lotus headquarters at Ketteringham Hall, a magnificent building set in 40 acres of grounds, complete with a lake and associated wildlife. DeLorean was told that the USAAF's Eighth Air Force had occupied the building during the Second World War and it was once visited by 'Ike' Eisenhower. After the war Ketteringham Hall became a preparatory school and was finally purchased by Colin Chapman in 1967.

The darker side of the relationship between John

DeLorean and Colin Chapman began in October 1978, in Geneva, when the plan to divert DeLorean funds was hatched. Jaroslav 'Jerry' Juhan, representing GPD (General Products Development), and his wife Marie-Denise Juhan Perrin were the innocent transacting partners for the DeLorean/Lotus deal. Colin Chapman and John DeLorean made an arrangement with GPD which was investigated later in the DeLorean programme by Sir Kenneth Cork in the UK and the IRS in the USA.

Colin Chapman demanded that DeLorean payments for development of the car were made in the most tax-effective manner, in the process protecting Lotus from the potential terminal effects of US product liability lawsuits. Any single liability claim could finish Lotus within weeks. Chapman argued that GPD was introduced as a partner in the deal to install a fusible link between DeLorean Motor Cars Ltd and Lotus in the event of litigation associated with the design integrity of the car. That was reasonable enough, but $17.65 million of payments to GPD undoubtedly went walkabout. Some of the money would never be located.

The main GPD contract was not a secret affair, as is generally thought. It was a written agreement, thrashed out over days in the President Wilson hotel in Geneva between John DeLorean and Colin Chapman. GPD, the DeLorean Research Partnership and DeLorean Motor Cars Ltd were the contracting parties. The arrangement was known to everyone involved in the DeLorean programme – not only John DeLorean, Colin Chapman and Fred Bushell, but the directors of DMC (the parent of DMCL), the management of NIDA and the Department of Commerce in Belfast.

The GPD contract was subject to intense discussion at NIDA and the Department of Commerce. Finally, on 19 October 1978, the civil servants decided that it was an operational matter and the responsibility of the DeLorean companies. NIDA's only concern was that the project should meet the financial and timing requirements of the corporate plan; the GPD contract, they argued, was not a matter that required the sanction of the government or civil servants.

John DeLorean was therefore free to make arrangements as he thought fit. He had been let loose.

A clause in the GPD document stated that Lotus Cars would undertake the design of the car. A separate letter from Lotus to GPD agreeing to undertake the activity would cause problems for Colin Chapman four years later. Payment terms for the contract were generous: $8.5 million to be paid immediately, with a further $1 million each quarter in 1979. An additional $5.15 million would be paid to GPD on the signing of the contract for the development of VARI. None of the money found its way to the development of the car or the plastic process. Lotus was ultimately paid £11 million over and above these amounts.

In the deal Lotus made it clear that they were only responsible for the design and durability of the car and not for the quality or production engineering activities. These were to be the responsibility of the DeLorean personnel at the factory in Belfast.

Colin Spooner, who had left Lotus a few years earlier, was brought back as the man in charge of engineering the DMC12. Colin directed a staff of 370 based in Factory 6, with more engineers in the main office complex at Hethel.

In early December 1978 a meeting held at Ketteringham Hall reviewed the Lotus report of Bill Collins's prototype undertaken by the Hethel engineering staff just weeks earlier. Not only was the report highly critical of the vehicle but, adding insult to injury, Colin Chapman was openly contemptuous of the prototype and used the report to demand that design of the car should start afresh. This time Lotus engineers would carry out the design work. From now on Bill Collins and his team were out of the programme; they would not be involved in any engineering activity on the car.

Two years after the collapse of DMCL I joined Lotus Cars as supplies director. As a mere mortal and not one of God's chosen few (that is, not an engineer), working with Lotus engineers was inspiring and frustrating in equal amounts, but it was never boring. The company was superbly led by Mike Kimberley, whose sole involvement in the DeLorean deal was to oversee engineering activity on the car. Mike saved Lotus from extinction after the death of Colin Chapman in 1982 and the furore that followed the DeLorean venture. That the company exists today is credit to him alone. Mike was an inspiring leader, who taught me and many other senior managers and directors at Lotus that loyalty is a two-way street.

*Chapter 6*

# THE FIRST YEAR

The purchasing office that I'd been employed to run opened in February 1979. Its location at Spire House, in the centre of Coventry, was ideal. Coventry is right in the middle of England, close to Birmingham International airport, and there was an abundance of automotive suppliers within a two-hour car drive of the office.

For the next two years I travelled to Lotus every week, staying for one or two days, then going to the plant in Dunmurry, and finally returning to the Coventry office on Friday, if at all possible. That's the way the average week was planned, anyway. At the peak of activity I employed 14 purchasing staff, all working on the production parts procurement programme – nominating suppliers, initiating tool manufacture, co-ordinating design changes with suppliers, arranging sample submissions and progressing approvals.

Every working day, from March 1979 to the handover of the programme by Lotus in November 1980, purchasing had a presence at Lotus Cars in Norfolk. All meetings with suppliers were minuted and follow-up action was noted. Drawings marked 'for discussion only' were ferried back daily to the Coventry office, which was open seven days a week for most weeks of the year.

Back in Belfast, recruitment was steaming ahead at full blast for supervisors, quality control operatives, and industrial and production engineers. Although Northern Ireland has a substantial history of engineering, technical innovation and manufacture there has never been a car industry of any size within the province. Only a few companies had ever made cars in Northern Ireland – the Chamber Motor Company in 1929, the Crossle Car Company made racing cars, and after the Second World War shipbuilders Harland and Wolff, makers of the RMS *Titanic*, manufactured the Nobel 200 Bubble car. In the 1960s Triumph Heralds were made from CKD kits (completely knocked down); the parts were assembled by Clarence Engineering, but this process soon became uneconomical.

Consequently, individuals with appropriate car-related technical experience were imported from the car manufacturing areas of England. The manufacturing department at Dunmurry soon became peppered with immigrants from England, attracted by the exciting new DeLorean venture and a higher than average pay packet, together with a generous relocation package.

There were many suppliers wanting to become involved in the DeLorean project. Some had been nominated by Bill Collins and his team prior to DeLorean setting up shop in Northern Ireland. These included Harrison Radiator, the supplier of the air-conditioning system; AC Spark Plug, who made the instrument cluster; Saginaw for the steering column; Delco Remy for the battery; and all divisions of General Motors. Another key supplier, Grumman Aerospace, had completed significant work on the roof structure. This included the torsion bars to which the gull wing doors would be attached.

During my first visit to Lotus, in early January 1979, I met Colin Spooner, the man in charge of the development programme for the DeLorean car. The trip had another purpose, which was to meet the Grumman team who were visiting Lotus and had arranged their travel itinerary to coincide with John DeLorean's visit to Hethel. Grumman planned to present their design of the roof structure for the DMC12 to John DeLorean and other key Lotus staff. They were to be disappointed. John was in deep conversation with Colin Chapman and Mike Kimberley, a meeting lasting most of the day. Eventually John broke off for a few minutes to meet the visitors and shook hands with those around him.

'John DeLorean,' he said, as he moved his arm out to shake my hand. He clearly didn't remember my face from our brief meeting in Belfast in early December.

Art August led the team from Grumman, a man who was impressive and enthusiastic. This was further evidence, if it were needed, that the DeLorean programme had respectability and credibility, with global giants such as GM and Grumman both seeking a slice of our little venture. Although we had an overwhelming feeling of reverence and admiration for the Grumman visitors, with their slick presentation, complete with drawings, sketches and calculations, there was one thing that caused a slight distraction. The visitors were dressed in a manner that we country boys could only describe as an out-take from the gangster scene of the film *Some Like It Hot* – well-oiled shiny hair, combed straight back, mohair overcoats but alas no violin cases. We were not used to such an overpowering presence.

The Grumman team left Lotus that day after just a brief meeting with the great man. The only part of their roof structure design that would find its way on to the DMC12 would be the cryogenically twisted torsion bar. Eventually this would be made in Coventry, at SPS Industries. DMCL spent $178,000 for the twisting machine itself and another $36,000 for tooling. Possibly the figures included a premium for injury to feelings.

On that first trip to Lotus I was introduced to other members of Bill Collins's team who had worked on the prototype cars. Initially they were based at Ketteringham Hall, the home of Group Lotus and the Formula 1 team headquarters. They were now eager to move a mile down the road to Hethel in order to become involved in the day-to-day development of the DMC12, but they had only been granted restricted access. It became clear that the Collins and Lotus teams were not gelling and barely talking. We thought the reason for the conflict was that the Collins team regarded Lotus and the local DeLorean staff as incapable of engineering their baby into production and lacking the appropriate volume production experience. The real reason for the conflict was much simpler. Lotus had been advised to take instructions on engineering and design matters from John DeLorean alone, and to accommodate the American team as best they could, although in all other respects they were to be ignored. The relationship between the two parties became fraught, the atmosphere electric. We saw very little of the young Americans after late January 1979.

I didn't view the DeLorean prototypes as a product ready to be converted into a production vehicle, as Mike Loasby had thought when he took the job as engineering director. They were more like concept cars, of the type that's seen at motor shows, looking attractive but with no real engineering applied to the vehicle. Additionally, the car was to be engineered and redesigned from top to bottom to facilitate the VARI plastic body, with a fixed chassis frame and the interior restyled from scratch. It was on this basis that I thought 18 months to production was not possible. The outer door panel tooling alone would take a minimum of 18 months to complete from the time the design was approved, and this was yet to start. Pilot and pre-production runs would equate to 24 months for production parts for the main body panels; 36 months from January 1979 to the start of production was a good estimate. That would equate to a pre-production build in January 1982, 18 months later than planned.

John DeLorean had promised the government pre-production cars in July 1980 and he was not budging from this impossible timescale. It was forbidden to talk of any other date – regardless of logic.

In the early 1980s Jaguar Cars published a document advising all engineering staff of lead times for their new limousine, the XJ40. The document covered the complete range of parts required to build a car. A major body panel was quoted as taking just over 36 months from design release to production. We were given less than 18 months for the same type of tooling.

To assist in the development of the stainless steel body dies, Ted Chapman (no relation to Colin Chapman) was hired to assist in the design and progress of the tools. Ted, who had worked at Ford UK and Standard Triumph, was a pure professional and a great asset to the programme, but he often carried his heart on his sleeve. More than once he was taken aside by colleagues in an attempt to calm him down during project meetings at Lotus. Ted brought a significant amount of knowledge to the programme, his co-ordination of technical aspects of the tools being the reason why so many long lead-time body dies were made in such a short period. Although not always easy to accommodate, Ted made a major contribution to the DeLorean development programme. He liaised with tool makers in Germany – Lapple, Northelfer and Allgaier – and Lapple's pressing plant at Carlow.

Regular project meetings at Lotus commenced in early February 1979. They were held every two weeks, but as activity increased this schedule was altered to every week, on a Wednesday. We met at Lotus Factory 6, the former USAAF administration building. To allow efficient use of everyone's time a private charter plane was organised to fly the DeLorean team from Belfast to Norwich. The flight from Aldergrove airport, Belfast, operated by Woodgate Aviation, took off at 7am for Norwich airport, with a journey time of two-and-a-half hours. Usually the passenger list consisted of Chuck Bennington, George Broomfield, Shaun Harte, Barrie Wills, Mike Loasby, Tony Potter (then manufacturing manager) and myself (if I was in Belfast on the day of the flight; otherwise I'd drive from my home in

England). As the months passed other passengers hitching a ride included Joe Daly, finance director, and Ken Gorf, the company treasurer; they had temporary offices at Lotus. Usually seven or eight of us took the weekly flight to the joint meetings at Lotus. Barrie Wills chaired the sessions.

As a young man witnessing the events associated with the birth and growth of a new company, working with such big names from the automotive industry was fascinating and educational but sometimes amusing. As the months ticked by various factions appeared at the senior level within the company. Some directors were on good terms, others would prefer to avoid speaking. This was clearly demonstrated by their actions when we were preparing to board the plane for the journey home from Lotus. Directors would jockey for position in the queue to climb the steps and be the first to board the tiny aircraft that would hold a maximum of eight passengers, one seat either side of the aisle. Sometimes a person would be wanting to avoid sitting next to someone else, so one or two would make their way to the front of the queue in order to be able to occupy the only seat without a corresponding adjacent seat, or take a seat next to a friendly face. As the junior in the team I would, of course, board last, so inevitably the only vacant seat would be adjacent to a bad-tempered and cantankerous individual whom everyone else was avoiding. This ritual occurred time and time again.

One of the actions from the joint project meetings with Lotus was for my team to choose a development partner for a particular item or process. Although Lotus was experienced in automotive engineering they were not, as they admitted, experts in the design of mass production components. Our immediate priority was to identify suitable business partners for the parts requiring major investment. The front and rear fascias, chassis frame and stainless steel panels were examples of where assistance from a knowledgeable supplier was essential from the start. The list of nominated suppliers grew as the engineering and development programme gathered pace.

The early involvement of suppliers was to ensure that Lotus designed a part that would be fully compatible to meet the requirements of a particular process and wouldn't require redesign when the part was finally sourced. Suppliers had to be nominated at an early stage. The process would save time and engineering costs but caused significant disagreement within the company.

The process of involving a supplier at the early stages is now referred to as 'simultaneous engineering' – a workflow that involves working in parallel through stages. For example, commencing tool design before the design of the product was finished or procuring the steel tool block from the design concept before the part had been designed saved considerable time. Although this does not reduce the amount of manpower required for a project, it does drastically reduce lead times. We didn't realise that this was the manufacturing and procurement process of the future, to be followed by most European car manufacturers; we just thought it made sense.

We took drawings from Lotus marked 'for discussion purposes only' to issue to potential suppliers. From the results of our enquiry we would choose a supplier to assist Lotus in the development of the part. These were chosen on ability and track record rather than price. We were a new company, with new staff, and Lotus demanded mature vendors, not beginners. There was enough risk in the business already without introducing further concerns.

Suppliers needed to possess the technical ability to design products that satisfied US Federal requirements and to test accordingly. Legal requirements for automotive parts were constantly changing and becoming more complicated by the day. It was essential to have a supplier's support and expertise from the commencement of design of a product or part. For example, the US SAE standard on 'Vehicular Traffic Sound Signalling Devices' (i.e. horns) function and design directive contains over 2,000 words. By comparison, the Ten Commandments given by God on Mount Sinai contained 123 words. How we have progressed over the centuries.

In early March Arthur Andersen, the company's auditors, began their review of DMCL's annual accounts. They approved the accounts but failed to spot the missing $17.65 million GPD money. Four years later action would be taken against Arthur Andersen for their failure to identify the alleged fraud. The UK government argued that this omission had led them to continue further investment in DMCL – in what was then otherwise regarded as a risky but honest programme.

By mid-March 1979 Bill Collins had left the company and joined AMC (eventually to become partly owned by Renault). Gene Cafiero joined in May 1979. At first he made few visits to the plant, mainly for board meetings, and then returned to the USA or to Lotus. Later in the programme, towards production, he was present most of the time at Dunmurry.

John DeLorean's visits to Lotus, accompanied by Gene and Chuck, were certainly similar to royal events, with everything tidy and in its place. There was an element of Lotus Esprits being wheeled out of the workshops and DeLorean cars wheeled in during these visits, but not to the degree that has been suggested by some commentators. If the amount of work and effort put in by Lotus on the DeLorean car had been to the level that is suggested by some, then the car would have taken more time than the actual 22 months it took to complete. Serious work on the car commenced at Lotus in February 1979 and it was completed by early December 1980, an amazing achievement which required dedicated effort by Colin Spooner and his team.

With over 700 people employed in the construction process, building at the plant was going well, if not ahead of schedule. Then disaster struck: the company contracted to supply the steel structure for the body shop got into financial difficulties and entered receivership. Building work came to a halt on that part of the plant. In an attempt to get construction back on course Dixon Hollinshead visited the parent company of the contractor at Hull, in Yorkshire. Although most of the steel was available the company, now under the direction of the receiver, demanded significantly higher prices before releasing the steel to Belfast. After all, John DeLorean had been given £54 million so why not take a slice? Dixon was far too experienced in business to tolerate this. He abruptly terminated the meeting, packed his briefcase and said: 'Not to worry, I'll get the steel from Korea.' The atmosphere changed and serious negotiations then began. The steel was shipped at the right price, although a little later than originally planned.

The shadow Northern Ireland Secretary, Airey Neave, came to the plant in mid-February 1979. He was a key member of Margaret Thatcher's Conservative party and a close personal friend of the future Prime Minister. Thirty years earlier, during the Second World War, Airey Neave had been one of the few successful escapees from the infamous Colditz prisoner of war camp in Germany. Also, as a fluent German speaker and lawyer, he prosecuted at the Nuremberg trials in 1945–46. Chuck Bennington and Dixon Hollinshead led his tour around the DeLorean site, then still just a muddy field. Six weeks later, on 30 March 1979, Airey Neave's booby-trapped car exploded outside the Houses of Parliament in London; he died in the wreckage. His death, according to some, conditioned Margaret Thatcher to a distaste of all things associated with Northern Ireland from that day forward.

By March 1979 most of the ground site had been cleared, except for one small area behind the assembly building area where a 'faery tree' grew. No Irishman would contemplate harming such a tree as to do so would result in lifelong misery for the individual and their family. Dixon made it known that he had buried £200 under the roots and the money could be kept by anyone removing the tree. Days afterwards the tree disappeared. (It is noticeable, of course, that although it was an easy task Dixon didn't remove the tree himself. Some years later there was a report that the man who'd done the job had lost a limb in an industrial accident.)

On the commercial front, Frank McCann wrote to the company's solicitor, Robin Bailie, on 12 April conveying a formal offer from the Department of Commerce detailing financial assistance for the DeLorean venture. The total package, including grants, loans and equity, totalled £53 million. The 11-page offer was accepted by Myron Stylianides and John DeLorean on 9 May.

In June John DeLorean and the Lotus team reviewed the styling of the car and decided that it was beginning to look dated, tired and needed to be refreshed. New styling lines were agreed with Giugiaro. Details were passed to Visioneering in Detroit to start work on new body stacks to be used in the design and manufacture of the body dies.

Work on the new body master at Visioneering had to go back to the beginning because of the restyling, but the date for the start of pilot production at Dunmurry remained unchanged – a year later, in July 1980 – and therefore we now had less than a year to complete, validate and prove body panels, a process that would normally take three years. Thanks to Ted Chapman, Colin Spooner, Visioneering and the die-makers, the task was completed in just 19 months.

As the summer drifted by we settled into a routine: weekly meetings at Lotus, regular meetings with suppliers and, of course, our regular monthly meetings with Renault. It was on returning from one of these meetings in Paris in late August that I noticed a headline in the newspapers – 'Mountbatten Killed' in the Republic of Ireland and 18 soldiers dead at Warren Point in Northern

▲ *Twinbrook fields prior to work beginning on the 72-acre DeLorean site. The faery tree stands alone midfield near the brook.* (Matt Sommer)

▼ *John DeLorean speaking to the press in the training building at the official launch of DeLorean Motor Cars Ltd on 4 October 1978.* (Matt Sommer)

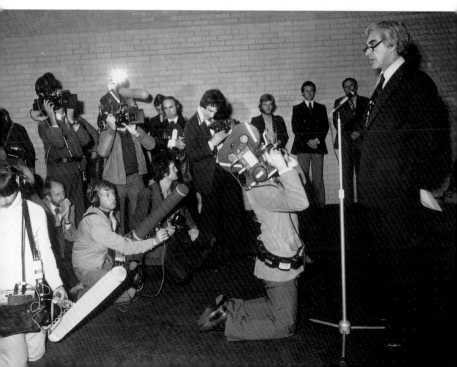

▲ *The reception area of the training building. The stairs led to the boardroom and directors' offices.* (Tony Swann)

▼ *Children from the Twinbrook estate dwarfed by one of the giant earthmovers. This photograph was taken on the day of the groundbreaking ceremony: 4 October 1978. Local child John Costello is on the left.* (Matt Sommer)

▲ *A copper plaque on a stone base was laid to commemorate the groundbreaking. From left: Lou Glasgow, Dick Brown, Barbara Hollinshead, Lesley Jenkins, Myron Stylianides and Dixon Hollinshead.* (Matt Sommer)

▼ *This photograph was taken at Lotus Cars. From left: Michael Kimberley, managing director of Group Lotus; Colin Spooner, who was in charge of the development and engineering of the DeLorean car; John DeLorean; and Peter Wright, managing director of Lotus Engineering.* (Robert Lamrock)

▲ This photograph of the USAAF 389th Heavy Bomb Group Administration block was taken around 1944; 20 years later these buildings became known as Lotus factory 6. The DeLorean car was designed in these buildings by Colin Spooner's team from early 1979 to late 1980. (2nd Air Division Memorial Library collection)

▲ Lotus factory 6 in the mid-1980s. The building has changed very little over 40 years. Today it is home to Lotus Classic Cars. (Neil Phillipson collection, 2nd Air Division Memorial Library)

▼ The USAAF site at Hethel, eventually to become home for Lotus Cars. The aircraft hangar in the background was refurbished by Lotus to facilitate the building of Moonraker boats; afterwards it became the development area for the DeLorean car. (2nd Air Division Memorial Library collection)

▲ *A photograph of Ketteringham Hall taken in 1944–5 when the building was occupied by USAAF staff – note the stars and stripes flag.* (2nd Air Division Memorial Library collection)

▼ *Bob Dance, Colin Chapman's chief mechanic, took this photograph of Ketteringham Hall in the early 1980s when the building was home to Team Lotus and Group Lotus, the Formula 1 company owned by Colin Chapman.* (Bob Dance)

▲ *Colin Chapman's sitting room at Ketteringham Hall, December 1978. The topic was Lotus's review of Bill Collins's prototype known as Doris 1a. From left: Chuck Bennington, Bill Collins, Colin Chapman, John DeLorean, Fred Bushell and Michael Kimberley.* (Tony Swann)

▼ *Doris 1a in the refurbished USAAF hangar. The red DeLorean in the background is Doris 3 (Pilot 3).* (Paul Fricker)

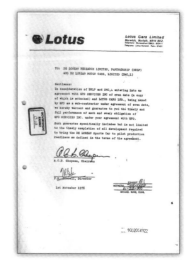

▲ *One of three versions of the GPD contract. John DeLorean and Marie Denise Juhan, who were representing GPD, signed this, which is the only signed version.* (Matthew Harte)

▲ *This memo links Group Lotus to GPD. Colin Chapman failed to include the revenue from GPD in Group Lotus accounts until late 1982, when the Inland Revenue began investigating the company.* (Matthew Harte)

▼ *Paul Fricker, Lotus engine development engineer, in Yuma, Arizona on hot-climate-testing duty with Doris 9 (Pilot 9).* (Paul Fricker)

▲ *Doris 20 and Doris 21 Pilot cars arrive in the US for EPA evaluation. Peter Allison (who represented DMCL and John Bloomfield Lotus Cars) is on the left opening a box of spares while Paul Fricker took the photograph.* (Paul Fricker)

▼ *A publicity photograph of (from left) Chuck Bennington, Barrie Wills and George Broomfield with a PRV engine.* (Robert Lamrock)

Ireland. That date, 27 August 1979, was a black day for mankind and there would be many more.

In October we learned that John had purchased Logan Manufacturing, a snow-grooming company in Utah. The news was received by us with some bewilderment. We made sports cars so exactly what was a snow-grooming machine and where was Utah? A few years after John's arrest we learned how he had funded the capital to buy Logan Manufacturing from Thiokol Chemical Company, one of the major players in the US chemical industry.

Around this time Bill Haddad was appointed vice president in charge of planning. Bill appeared in Belfast shortly after his appointment. He was co-operative, likeable and always had a moment to spare for those working in the factory, regardless of rank. These might have been the traits of a seasoned communications guru but it didn't matter; we liked him and we thought he liked us.

Bill's credentials were the envy of anyone working at DeLorean in New York. He had been a confidant of the Kennedy family, one of the founders of the Peace Corps, and also acted as associate director and inspector general of that body under John F. Kennedy. He had also worked as an assistant to Robert Kennedy in his presidential campaign. He made many friends both in the company and the locality, particularly Twinbrook; he talked to directors, management and those paid hourly. He was to be seen in journalistic suspenders (i.e. braces), typing his reports for hour after hour and staring out of the training room window towards the factory block, possibly searching for inspiration.

In November John's book *On a Clear Day You Can See General Motors* was published. We were surprised to read its criticism of one of our major suppliers. General Motors was responsible for the air-conditioning unit, instrument cluster, steering column, battery and other parts; all were critical and not replaceable at this stage in the programme, and all were being supplied by the car super-giant.

The book was released at a time when we were demanding the full support of the supply base. How would they react? Why release the book now? Any disruption could potentially kill the DeLorean dream, if executives at GM took offence. There was a rush to buy a copy, if only in an attempt to answer any questions that might arise and assess the damage. This self-inflicted wound would be the first of many that we witnessed during the life of the DeLorean programme. Fortunately GM executives chose to ignore John's book, so life continued, albeit with a huge sigh of relief.

Winston Churchill once said of John Foster Dulles, one-time US Secretary of State, 'He's a bull who carries his own china shop around with him.' This could equally apply to John DeLorean. His later slips and accidents of timing would prove fatal for the company.

## Chapter 7

# THE SUPPLIERS
# AND THE PROCESSES

Why John DeLorean agreed a deal with a South American company to supply the stainless steel body panels and dies we will never know. A contract for the business was promised to a Brazilian manufacturer long before John arrived in Northern Ireland. After Belfast was chosen as the manufacturing site the logistics of a Brazilian supply-chain operation for the provision of a multitude of stainless steel parts loaded on to pallets was explained to John DeLorean – namely, that a critical supplier located 3,000 miles from the plant was less than ideal. He understood the problem and allowed us to localise the business in Europe.

Due to the complexity and tight timescale of the DeLorean programme, easy communications and a close locality of the chosen vendor for the dies and panels were essential. Northern Ireland didn't have a supplier of this type, but there was one in the Republic of Ireland: August Lapple GmbH, the Irish manufacturing arm of a German parent. The company had significant experience in the manufacture of dies and pressings for the automotive industry, and it was located in Carlow, just 150 miles by road from Dunmurry.

There were two problems in finalising the deal

with Lapple. The first was their concern regarding the financial exposure required to support the DeLorean programme when in full production. This problem was answered by reducing Lapple's bills by supplying pre-cut stainless panels on a free-issue basis directly to them from BSC (British Steel Corporation). DMCL paid BSC for the steel delivered to Lapple, who in turn invoiced only labour and overheads to DMCL, hence reducing Lapple's exposure.

The second issue was the significant investment required for Lapple's Carlow plant to purchase and install the additional presses and associated facilities for the DeLorean business, an investment they were not prepared to fund entirely from their own pocket. Lapple applied for grant aid to the Ministry of Trade, Commerce and Tourism; this was headed by Des O'Malley who, a year earlier, had thrown out the DeLorean deal on behalf of the Irish government. Grant money was eventually awarded, however. Thus the two problems were resolved and the programme commenced.

In the early discussions with Lapple it was realised that they didn't possess the die-making capacity to manufacture all the dies in the lead times required for the DeLorean programme. To resolve this issue two additional die-makers were contracted to take up the extra capacity. Allgaier GmbH were awarded contracts for the rear quarter dies, Northelfer GmbH were to supply the front fenders and Lapple supplied the balance of the tools. In total, DMCL paid £3.2 million for the 33 stainless steel pressings specified for the car. When completed, the dies were shipped to Lapple in Carlow for manufacture of the pressings, which in turn would be supplied to Dunmurry.

The second casualty of the DeLorean European localisation programme after the Brazilian body-die deal was cancelled was the ERM process (Elastic Reservoir Moulding). Bill Collins had originally chosen ERM for the body structure, but following evaluation of the early DeLorean prototype Lotus opined that ERM was unlikely to have sufficient rigidity and strength for the car's structure; also, that the process was untried in a production vehicle and therefore posed a risk.

John DeLorean was convinced by Colin Chapman's arguments. Also, as the complete body structure would be assembled from various parts, this would in turn reduce the overall integrity and rigidity of the structure. This was unlike VARI, Lotus argued, where the body is moulded in two pieces astride a single-piece chassis frame – a system tried and tested on production vehicles, albeit in low volumes. (As mentioned earlier, the VARI process was originally developed at Lotus for the Moonraker brand of boat hulls and was then used successfully for the Lotus Eclat sports car, produced at a rate of three per day.)

Choosing VARI for the body brought an additional financial bonus: the royalty payment of $5.15 million for the licence arrangement would be paid directly to GPD. This money was part of the $17.65 million later described by Sir Kenneth Cork, the receiver, as having gone walkabout.

In production, the DeLorean VARI body was made in two halves – an upper and lower moulding, weighing at birth 54kg and 85kg respectively. The two halves were bonded with Goodyear Pliogrip to complete the shell assembly; the joint line between the two halves was overlapped with glass fibre to secure the assembly.

VARI had advantages over ERM. Capital expenditure for moulds was significantly lower, while modifications, particularly the changes anticipated in the early stages of production, would be more easily accommodated than those of a steel tool, which ERM demanded.

ERM did have benefits over VARI, however, including less manufacturing space; labour content would be lower by far; and cooling ovens and fettling booths would not be required. These two processes alone would take up half of the body-shop manufacturing area and add a significant amount of labour cost.

The overriding problem with ERM was the capital investment for the three or four huge hydraulic presses required at Dunmurry and the steel tooling required for the process. In total, an additional £10 million would be needed to fund the capital expenditure, money we didn't have. As there was still some debate over the long-term use of ERM, the body-shop building at Dunmurry was built with high bays to accommodate the large presses required in any change to future policy.

Later in the life of the DeLorean programme there was a plan to extend the building and change to ERM in order to allow higher volumes of bodies to be made from the same space. It wouldn't be difficult to guess who would be asked to pay for the investment.

The expected life of a VARI tool set (there were 12 sets when in full production) was 2,000 shots for the female tool and 1,000 for the male tool before major maintenance was required. At weekends selective VARI tools were taken out of service for modifications to accommodate engineering changes. As the maintenance area had limited resources only two or three moulds could be modified or repaired in any one weekend; this resulted in various revision levels of VARI tools being used at any one time.

All was not lost for ERM, however, because it was to find its way on to the DMC12 via the rear closing panel, front fascia reinforcement and the rear licence-plate bezel. The parts were supplied by Composite Technology Corporation in Detroit, part of the DeLorean group of companies.

To produce 80 cars per day the body shop worked a three-shift system, the maximum that could be shoehorned from the site using the VARI process.

One contract signed by John DeLorean before the Belfast deal was agreed did hold up well, and this was the agreement with Renault for the supply of the engine and gearbox. It was signed long before Northern Ireland had been suggested as a manufacturing base. The commercial package was later adapted to reflect the company's location at Dunmurry. The 2.85-litre PRV engine was made at Douvrin in northern France and the gearbox at Renault's facility near Caen in Normandy, and these locations were close enough to allow weekly shipments by sea from France to Northern Ireland. Although the contract was agreed with DRM (Division Renault Moteurs) the financials were underwritten by COFACE, the French equivalent of the British Export Credit Guarantee Board. Payment terms were favourable, with 120 days' payment guaranteed by John DeLorean personally.

Other car manufacturers supplied parts and components for the DMC12. General Motors supplied off-the-shelf parts but also developed custom-made components manufactured to Lotus designs. The air-conditioning unit made by Harrison Radiator, a division of GM, utilised some parts supplied to other GM car manufacturers, with Lotus-designed add-on mouldings to adapt the standard product to the DMC12. Saginaw provided the steering column; Delco Remy the battery; Rochester Products parts for the emissions; AC Spark Plug the instrument cluster.

The instrument cluster was changed significantly from the early prototypes. One of my first tasks, early in the programme, was to visit AC Spark Plug in Flint, Michigan, to discuss changes to the layout of the panel. Eventually we agreed a revised layout of the warning lights and main dials. The tooling costs associated with the change amounted to well over $500,000.

General Motors were one of the top-performing suppliers to the Dunmurry facility. Their attention to detail, quality awareness and supply performance, including timescale of delivery and engineering support, were all of the highest standard.

Hills Precision in Coventry, a division of Chrysler Corporation, were awarded the contract for the instrument shroud assembly. The part was one of the most complex and difficult components made for the car. Producing a vacuum-formed ABS skin in a foam mould with a metal support structure caused untold misery to all who attempted to make good parts from the process. The early cars assembled at Dunmurry during the pre-production training period in 1980 used hand-stitched instrument shrouds, as the production process at Hills Precision refused to comply with normal manufacturing rules of compliance; the first production run of shrouds from Hills was supplied in mid-January 1981. Six months earlier, in late summer 1980, knowing that this process would continue to be a problem, we allocated a DeLorean representative full-time from the purchasing team to be located at Hills Precision; this was not only to assist in the co-ordination process with the engineers at Hills but also to maintain the morale of production staff who believed that the product was impossible to make. Eventually Hills succeeded in converting our investment of £39,000 into acceptable parts.

Rearsby Automotive, a division of British Leyland, supplied the pedal box and gearshift pressings. Ivor Vaughan, the managing director, was a passionate supporter of the DeLorean programme and became involved in any issue that threatened to blemish the good name of his company.

The multitude of trim components designed for the car required a different approach. To procure the parts from separate suppliers was not a feasible operation. To overcome this logistical problem, a joint venture between DMCL and Chamberlain and Phipps Ltd, based in Northampton in England, was conceived, with the former taking 51% of the new venture. The new company, Trimtech, was based just five miles from Dunmurry.

The wiring harness was developed between Lotus and Rists Wires and Cables (a division of Lucas Industries); Rists was one of the three resident suppliers of car wiring in the UK and the only vendor that showed any interest in the DeLorean programme. In mid-1981, at the behest of John DeLorean, we discussed the transfer of this business to Packard Wiring in Dublin. By the time our plans had been concluded for the transfer of the business to Packard, however, DMCL had entered receivership.

Phoenix GmbH supplied the reinforced resin injection mouldings known as RRIM. Other companies were considered, but as Phoenix enjoyed a history of making similar parts for Porsche and other high-performance vehicles we chose them as the supplier for all the exterior mouldings. Phoenix gave the lead in engineering and development of the parts. Time would be the judge of their expertise, particularly as the front fascia distorted badly from the heat generated from the headlights, a problem which only showed up after cars had been in service for some time. A lack of long-term field development trials didn't assist either.

I don't suppose it is that often that the manufacturing process of beer barrels is discussed in a car development programme, but this was the case at Lotus in early 1979 during one of the first joint DMCL/Lotus project reviews. We were considering stainless 304 for the chassis frame, the highest grade of the material available. But in the late 1970s the only mass-produced welded product using this grade of stainless was the standard beer barrel.

Lotus and DeLorean debated the use of stainless steel for the frame, but GKN, the chosen vendor, had concerns regarding the use of stainless, particularly its low-temperature impact properties and spring-back characteristics during the pressing process. They also had little or no knowledge of welding the material. The properties of mild steel were well known, but stainless steel had big question marks. So mild steel it was to be

– and to ensure it met the requirements of the ethical car, the chassis frame was hot dipped in a plastic resin.

In early 1979 the DeLorean purchasing team began a search for a variety of other products to satisfy the car's ethos of being corrosion resistant. A key item in the search was a fuel tank that met that criterion. In the late 1970s most car fuel tanks were constructed from mild steel, coated internally and externally. Our favourite option of the many variants reviewed was a blow moulding, although to our knowledge the only road vehicle to use a plastic tank at the time was the tiny Renault 4.

A stainless steel fabricated tank was dismissed for the same reasons as the material was discarded for the chassis frame – the unknown welding properties of stainless steel. We also dismissed a bladder-type fuel tank as used on helicopters; Firestone supplied samples and was interested in agreeing a development contract, but a protective shroud to hold the bladder would be necessary, thus making the assembly expensive.

Eventually DYNO Industries in Norway was chosen as the supplier of a blow-moulded fuel tank. This was an easy decision as they were the only supplier to understand the US requirements for chlorification, a process that restricted fuel permeating through the plastic walls of the tank.

Perhaps the best known of the new processes and materials used on the DeLorean was the cryogenically twisted door torsion bar. The product was developed by Grumman Aerospace as part of a roof-spider structure. Their original design included glass fibre and carbon fibre materials. But only the torsion bar found its way into production. To make the component, a stainless steel forged bar was twisted ten revolutions, then cooled in liquid nitrogen at minus 196°C. At this low temperature, the molecular structure of the bar is retained when the bar is cooled. The torsion bar acts as a hinge on the roof structure. When the door is closed the bar is twisted further and the energy now contained in the structure acts as a counter-balance to the weight of the 80lb door. It was a simple process, but we were fearful that this part would result in major warranty costs.

'Cryogenic' was a new word that we learned quickly and used as if we knew something more than the next man. It sat well with other phrases we had picked up when selling the project to potential suppliers, including terms such as 'austenitic stainless steel', 'chlorification' and 'RRIM'. But terminology was an issue from the beginning.

The US description of a car's parts compared to that used in Europe caused some confusion at the start, but we soon learnt to translate. The fascia is not the panel facing the driver but the front end of the vehicle; the sill becomes a rocker (but not one that rides a motorcycle). But when the boot is a trunk and the bonnet is both a hood and a trunk and therefore also a boot, things could become complicated. It's not surprising we got a few things wrong.

*Chapter 8*

# ONE STEP FORWARD, ONE STEP BACK

In early January 1980 Basil Wainwright – a colourful entrepreneur would be the kindest of descriptions – wrote to John DeLorean suggesting that we might be interested in a new invention he had developed: plasma ignition. The product was specifically designed to improve fuel efficiency in car engines. By late January his letter had filtered down to me. I was assigned to review the product and to organise a trip for Basil to visit Lotus. We met in late January. Unable to make progress in discussions, he suggested that his expert should visit Lotus the following week to discuss the merits of the system and review the engineering in detail. The meeting was held at Hethel; the conclusion by Lotus was, as expected, that there was no benefit in the system, only enormous development costs and a significant royalty payment to Basil. A report was submitted to John DeLorean concluding that plasma ignition had no benefits over orthodox systems and should be discarded.

John was never one to lose the chance to use a new phrase and an opportunity to impress his audience. Accordingly, on 20 February 1980, when he appeared on Ulster Television in Northern Ireland with the

Visioneering car that had been flown over from Detroit for the TV appearance, he proclaimed, without hesitation, the benefits of plasma ignition. He said that the system would be specified for the car and would dramatically reduce fuel consumption. It sounded wonderful, but of course it was nonsense; great public relations talk, perhaps, but those of us who had been involved in the research of plasma ignition knew it to be DeLorean speak. This was a phrase we had become accustomed to hearing throughout the short history of the company.

The evening after the television appearance the company held an open night for the 250 people then employed by DMCL. The employees could invite friends and relatives to the factory to see the progress that had been made since the groundbreaking ceremony. The event was held in the training building. The first prototype car from Visioneering in Detroit was there, transferred from the television studios earlier that day. The training building was full to bursting point that evening; everyone in the Belfast vicinity must have attended. It was difficult to move through the crowd, particularly in the area where John DeLorean was standing. Plans of the factory were there for everyone to see, with literature available to take home. The TV cameras were present and the local press were talking to the staff. I was in John's company and we started to talk, but before we got very far he put out his hand and said 'John DeLorean'. At this point I thought of replying 'Nick Sutton'.

During the evening I spoke to one of the DMCL security guards. I said that this was a great venture and asked for his opinion. Without a moment's hesitation he replied: 'It'll fail, everything in West Belfast does, look at all the things that are promised here. Only the risky ventures come to this part of the world. I'll be looking for another job very shortly.' How negative and depressing, I thought. Were these the comments and views of a seasoned West Belfast man or those of a visionary? I walked away to speak to someone who had a more positive attitude to life.

The next day the Secretary of State for Northern Ireland, Humphrey Atkins, toured the factory with his wife; the event was covered by the world's press. This was his first visit since he'd been appointed to the Northern Ireland job nine months earlier.

Three weeks after the open night in Dunmurry the BBC national news made an announcement that would haunt me for the next 30 years. On 11 March 1980 the body of Thomas Niedermayer was found in a shallow grave close to the DeLorean plant. He'd been kidnapped in December 1973 from his home in Glengoland in West Belfast, a mile or so from Dunmurry. Herr Dr Thomas Niedermayer was the managing director of Grundig GmbH and the West German honorary consul for Northern Ireland; his factory was only a stone's throw from the DeLorean site in Dunmurry. The Grundig facility employed over 800 people and was regarded as one of the success stories of NIDA.

The full story of his kidnap emerged years later. He had been lured from his house one night after one of his young daughters answered the door to the kidnappers. It was a few days after Christmas. He was taken and held hostage in a house in West Belfast. During a struggle to escape he was hit with the butt of a gun; the blow fractured his skull and he died immediately. His kidnappers buried him face down in a shallow grave not far from Dunmurry. For the next seven years his wife pleaded for his abductors to reveal the whereabouts of his body; the pleas were harrowing. How could any sane person not respond to this poor woman's request? Seven years after his abduction, following a tip-off to the police, Thomas Niedermayer's remains were found.

I watched the television news in the Conway hotel, opposite the Dunmurry factory, on the day of his funeral. His widow Ingeborg and their two daughters, Gabrielle and Renate, accompanied the body through the churchyard in Dunmurry with a dignity that could only be described as heroic. But the Niedermayer family were in such profoundly deep mourning at the time that further consequences would only follow years later.

Shortly after the funeral the Grundig factory closed with the loss of all 800 jobs, and the proposed new plant in Newry, planned for the following year, was scrubbed. The reason given for the closure of the Grundig plant was that competition from the Far East was causing a rethink of the economics of manufacture in Northern Ireland.

A significant number of the workers made redundant by the Grundig operation applied for work at the DeLorean plant. News of the discovery of Thomas Niedermayer's body disturbed some of the senior DeLorean staff as it rekindled concerns that they had buried regarding the dangers of working in Belfast. It also worried John DeLorean and provided a good reason why he should keep away from Northern Ireland and never stay overnight in Belfast again.

Progress was being made on both the car and the factory, but the first cars would certainly be appearing later than the September date now being given to the government. How we were to build cars by September wasn't explained – the stainless steel outer skins wouldn't be available until the end of the year, if not later. We were told that the production plan had now changed, in that there would not now be a pre-production or production pilot run. These pre-production runs usually sorted out the initial teething problems and were an essential part of any new car programme. Every manufacturing company undertakes a pilot or pre-production run for their products – not to do so would be commercial suicide – but we were to go into saleable product without pre-production trials.

As the months ticked by the specification of John DeLorean's ethical car was shaping up nicely. Stainless steel outer panels, a GRP sub-structure and an epoxy-coated chassis frame completed the line-up of corrosion-resistant components. In addition, a plastic fuel tank and polyurethane front and rear fascia panels added to the profile. The detail was not forgotten. CuNiFer brake pipes that wouldn't rust and petrol lines made from similar materials were specified. The concept was followed throughout the car's components.

All was well with the image, except for one thing. The claimed 27 miles per gallon used in marketing the ethical car through the DeLorean advertising programmes had, by June 1980, slowly but surely drifted down to 16 miles per gallon. Lotus reported that the latest prototype pilot D7 was reading significantly lower fuel consumption than even their worst nightmares had imagined.

The 'gas guzzler' law introduced by Congress in the USA imposed a penalty for all cars that failed to meet a minimum requirement, in DeLorean's case 22.6mpg. How could John DeLorean claim to be the maker of an ethical car when it failed even the minimum standards of fuel economy? There were punitive penalties for cars not meeting the standard. A fine of $5 per vehicle was imposed for every tenth of a mile per gallon that the car fell below the minimum level. Paying the fine was offered as a solution, but John DeLorean was having none of it. He was vehement in his response that the car should meet the EPA requirements. Reducing the weight of the car was one option; he offered a solution himself when he declared that many of the parts we had developed over the past year would become optional extras.

Paul Fricker, then a talented young engineer, worked on the PRV engine with Dennis Brown under guidance from Tony Rudd, engineering director of Lotus cars (known as 'Uncle Tony' by the staff at Lotus) tells the story. The Bill Collins team registered 27mpg during testing of the D1a prototype car. When Lotus tested the car for emissions and fuel consumption a problem was found that questioned earlier tests. The method of assessing fuel economy is determined at the tail pipe by collecting gases emitted from the exhaust. If the exhaust system is not fully sealed a false reading will result. The first DeLorean prototype (Doris 1a) leaked air into the pipe between the car's exhaust and the emission-measuring stem at the test house. This additional air in the exhaust gave the illusion of the car using less fuel in the test by reducing the concentration of $CO_2$. The actual economy level was much lower than originally thought. The pinhole in the welds of the prototype exhaust system resulted in false readings of exhaust gases on the emissions metering device.

Two emergency plans were instigated. The first was to undertake a 50,000-mile durability test. The second was the implementation of an engineering programme at Lotus to identify possible changes to the PRV engine and transaxle that would improve consumption.

Most new cars then sold in the USA undertook a 50,000-mile test for durability of components used in the fuel system and to confirm that the fuel usage had not deteriorated with use. Average speed was to be 30mph, with emission tests every 4,000 miles. For cars that were similar in weight and performance, piggy-backing the initial test and undertaking a 4,000-mile confirmation test to verify the results would be accepted; we had planned to go for the latter option in the engine development programme. It now looked likely that a 50,000-mile test would be required, a costly and time-consuming programme.

Barrie Wills, purchasing director of DeLorean and chairman of the joint DMC/Lotus development programme, summoned the key players to Belfast to discuss the issue. On Friday 13 June 1980 PRV representatives arrived at Dunmurry, Messrs Bertetto, Mellander and Gross holding discussions with Barrie and Mike Loasby to plan the way forward. A further meeting on 19 June at the Douvrin PRV manufacturing plant in

France was arranged to discuss various changes to the engine, in an attempt to at least achieve a result greater than the 22.6mph 'gas guzzler' level. Representing Lotus were Dennis Brown and Paul Fricker.

Paul Fricker recalls that work was undertaken on the advance curve on the distributor with the assistance of Malam Industries in England. Lowering the engine idle speed, reviewing the use of Peugeot camshafts that had less overlap, the possible use of the Peugeot exhaust manifold, changing the axle ratio, a review of air shroud injects – all things were considered. Pilot car D9 was hurriedly completed to undertake the work. It was driven to Bosch in Germany for review and appraisal. Shortly afterwards the car was flown to Arizona for hot-climate testing, complete with calibrated components. The testing of D9 and the 50,000-mile durability tests were now running in parallel and it would be some time before the results would be known.

*Chapter 9*

# DELAYS AND DIFFICULTIES

In late summer the purchasing team continued to supply parts to Dunmurry, knowing they would never be used on saleable products. The operators in the training building required parts to practise assembly methods. The parts had to look like the real thing so they could gain knowledge of the component and the associated build process. Production engineers required parts to write the build instructions; service part illustrators required parts to draw the sketches for assistance in aftermarket work instructions. But some senior staff criticised the process, suggesting that we should wait until a particular component was fully released and samples approved before allowing operators to train on assembly methods or, for that matter, let the parts loose for any reason. While the internal arguments continued at the senior level in the company, we continued to supply parts day after day, week after week. The recipients of the material were grateful and we ignored the critics.

In July 1980 Gene Cafiero announced to the world's press that the DeLorean's production date had been delayed to allow time for intensive training of the workforce and to complete the 50,000-mile fuel emissions test as demanded by EPA regulatory requirements. Although both reasons were true the real cause for the delay was much simpler; many parts had yet to be designed and the associated tooling started. Many of the heavy investment items, including the rear louvre, a massive SMC moulding, engine cover and front and rear fascia mouldings, were only half complete. Most stainless steel dies were not due for completion until late January 1981 and the inner door in late February, these parts being the critical path to series production. There were many other parts close behind.

The prototype programme at Lotus was not due to be completed for another five months. We had known for some time that production would not begin before the end of the year. Even then cars would only be part complete. Yet the government had been informed that pilot production was due to commence in autumn 1980. The date slipped, initially to November, then to the New Year. Dates would drift as the latest deadline approached. Month by month the government was teased with minor delays. Within the company we knew that cars could not be built until the New Year. This was our little secret.

We were running out of money, and suppliers were not being paid for tooling; if they stopped work the programme would be delayed further. Purchasing staff persuaded many suppliers to continue work in anticipation of money coming through, arguing that the government had invested so much by this stage that it was inevitable that they would continue to fund the project until production began. The purchasing staff became both the buyers and the salesmen for the DeLorean cause.

At the start of the venture it had been predicted that the cash would run dry in July 1980 – and this was perhaps the only forecast we achieved on time in the whole programme, accurate almost to the day. John DeLorean had no choice but to ask for more money from the government. The 400 staff at the plant held their breath, waiting for a response from the authorities. It was now public knowledge that we had run out of money, a fact that didn't help our relationship with the supply base who had yet to complete tooling for many, if not most, components. On 6 August Humphrey Atkins, Secretary of State for Northern Ireland, announced that a further £14 million in the shape of a repayable loan was to be made available to the company. He made it clear that was to be the end of government support, regardless of circumstances. The money came through on 11 September 1980.

This latest request tipped the scales of credibility between John DeLorean and the British civil servants. The venture, initially seen as a risky but worthwhile operation, was now viewed as parasitic. The relationship between the two sides was at a low ebb.

This was equally matched by John's relationship with his colleagues in the US, and the decline continued when DeLorean offered to loan the company money from his personal bank account. In return, the entire assets of the company would be signed over to him. There was considerable anger among those who had previously supported John's grand plans at 280 Park Avenue, DeLorean's headquarters in New York.

There was a time when Gene Cafiero and John DeLorean rarely spoke, their relationship becoming more fraught as the programme progressed. In one incident John DeLorean, Chuck Bennington and Gene Cafiero were in a helicopter travelling from the Battersea terminal in London to Lotus Cars, a journey by road of three hours, but just 40 minutes by chopper. As is usual in helicopters, the passengers (and the pilot) had headphones and a microphone to speak to and hear each other. The DeLorean team were in the rear seat, three in a row, with Chuck in the middle. The atmosphere was unusually icy, and it was apparent that Gene and John had argued some time earlier that day. John said to Chuck, through his microphone, 'Ask him [Gene] what are his plans after the Lotus trip?' Clearly Gene could hear, but Chuck repeated the question, albeit with some embarrassment: 'He said what are your plans after the Lotus trip?' Gene's reply was 'I heard him!' and with that he took off his headset. In public they tried a little harder to give the impression that they enjoyed a durable relationship.

A few weeks later there was some good news from the Lotus team working on the PRV engine at Hethel. They confirmed that the 50,000-mile durability programme was not now required as their development programme had broken the barrier on the fuel economy issue. The latest pilot car was registering a reading greater than the 'gas guzzler' minimum of 22.6mpg, as defined for the DMC12, allowing the piggy-back test of

4,000 miles to be used in the submission to the EPA. But it wasn't to be an easy task.

To allow certification by the EPA two pilot cars, D20 and D21, were despatched from Lotus to Olsen Engineering in the US on 5 October 1980. Peter Allison from DMCL and John Broomfield, the Lotus emissions expert, flew to the United States to meet the cars. But disaster struck when the cars failed the EPA tests, one marginally and the other by a significant amount. An autopsy revealed that the engine fuel systems had been damaged by airline ground staff: they had smelled petrol fumes and arranged for

. The tests at the EPA were therefore null and void and had to be repeated. On 19 November pilot car D19 was hurriedly commissioned and flown to the US to replace the vehicle that had failed by a substantial margin. At the next test the cars passed.

All that was now required to start production was the supply of the revised distributor from Bosch, the new part being critical to the improved mpg performance. Renault agreed to purchase the part from Bosch and fit the part to the engine – simple enough – but Renault's bureaucratic change control system demanded an extraordinary length of time to introduce any new part or change to the engine. On this occasion it was six to seven months. The solution was for DMCL to purchase the parts directly from Bosch and fit the new parts on the production line at Dunmurry until the Renault system could catch up and supply the new part on the engine received from Douvrin.

Most components were now in the process of being tooled for full production; many would be used in the assembly building. With the engine specification now fixed we could see that the timing of the first production vehicles would be early 1981. But we had no idea about the timing of the underbody being made in the body shop. The staff at Dunmurry had not yet managed to mould a complete VARI moulding using the Lotus-made tooling. It was a difficult process as the Cellier injection system to be used for production had not yet been commissioned, so the low-volume Lotus process route was used for the first mouldings. This involved the resin being dispensed from a one-tonne tank, with the catalyst mixed in the correct proportions in the pipeline to allow the mixture to harden at a uniform rate throughout the mould. To assist in the learning curve, Lotus personnel were present to make the first bodies. The body shop was far from complete, which was a major hindrance in fine-tuning the moulding process. Much of the site's exterior was also incomplete, with many ditches and trenches yet to be filled in.

Mick Weir had then been employed by Lotus for ten years, working at Hethel on the production of VARI mouldings for both cars and boats. He was one of the experts who had been seconded to Dunmurry to assist in the manufacture of the first bodies. The first attempt at moulding was made in late October 1980, towards midnight. It was cold and damp, and resin doesn't flow well in these conditions. The process was by trial and error; the man holding the Prodef resin injection gun was employed by the manufacturer of the equipment as he had the most experience of all those present. He knew how much resin to dispense, and at what rate the material should flow, and in which VARI mould injection ports to place the nozzle.

Having tried, without success, for many hours to mould a body the Prodef employee decided to take a break for a call of nature. As the inside toilets were not yet complete he decided to use the outside facility. Regrettably, as it was dark and there were no floodlights, he failed to notice an open ditch. He fell and seriously injured his leg. His cries for help were heard, and the DMCL and Lotus staff assisted him from the ditch, but his pleas to be taken to hospital were ignored as the staff demanded that the first body be made before daybreak. Unable to walk, he was placed in a wheelbarrow and wheeled alongside the exterior of the VARI mould and then back to the resin tank to allow the first moulding to be made. After another hour or so they were successful in making the first definitive production body; only then was the Prodef man taken to accident and emergency.

At last we were making progress, but it was a pity that the government and civil servants didn't see it that way. We were behind schedule and someone had to take the blame for the continual delays. Changes to the management structure had to be made. The first casualty was Chuck Bennington.

One wet Tuesday evening in Belfast in early October 1980, failing to navigate a sharp bend, Chuck crashed the Lotus Esprit he was driving. It hurtled through a hedge into an adjacent field. In the process he flipped the car on to its roof and, as a bonus, cut the fuel lines. Chuck suffered broken ribs, had a suspected punctured lung and was also covered in petrol. He was taken to the local hospital but discharged himself several hours later. At 7am the following morning he arrived at the Woodgate Aviation terminal at Aldergrove airport, ready to take the regular weekly two-and-a-half-hour flight to Lotus. He was in pain during the flight, and his condition deteriorated throughout the day. He was told by many of his colleagues that an unpressurised plane was perhaps not the best method of travelling while having a punctured lung, but he ignored us. The fact that he survived the flight and the day's discussions is one further testimony to a man who was determined to succeed. He would fight to the end.

Someone decided that John DeLorean should know about the incident. This was the beginning of the end for Chuck as managing director. Having worked long hours, and travelled regularly to the USA at weekends, leaving on a Friday evening and returning to work on a Monday morning, he was exhausted; Chuck had finished his shift as managing director.

A few weeks later, in mid-October 1980, the Pennebaker film crew hired by John to record the history of the DeLorean Company made their only visit to Lotus to record the final session of the joint DMCL and Lotus engineering meeting to be held at Hethel. These meetings usually took place in a small room at Lotus Factory 6 (the former USAAF administration building), but as the camera crew required extra space to set up their equipment we moved to a larger room in the same block. Two wooden garage doors were the backdrop so the scene looked untidy, not befitting a venture spending more than £50 million of UK public money. The meeting was brief, albeit at times heated. I completed my presentation in record time, avoiding any matters that could be seen as political in nature. I didn't want to be seen as either the star of the show or be recorded in perpetuity as the token idiot on the management team.

The Pennebaker crew then moved to Belfast to film the monthly board meeting. At one point during that meeting John became agitated at the apparent 'double dipping' of PRV into the DeLorean purse. With the cameras present, and wishing to retain his credibility, he berated Renault and PRV for their lack of understanding of the commercial realities of life. The debate related to the use of emission parts used on the Volvo 264, which DeLorean was now committed to using under the piggy-back EPA accreditation process. (We had to use the same parts as Volvo specified on cars sold in the USA so as to obtain equivalency for Federal emissions approval.) The parts in question were the catalytic convertor, lambda sensor and heat shields, all used on the Volvo 264. Unfortunately the supply contract for the DeLorean programme was contracted to Renault, but the parts in question were owned by Volvo who demanded a contribution towards their tooling and development costs.

This particular set of circumstances had not been foreseen when the contract with Renault was written and agreed by John DeLorean. Now John was playing to the gallery, but everyone around the table knew the problem was of his own making – hence the astonished looks when he'd finished speaking about inappropriate behaviour by PRV. Volvo eventually received £150,000 in compensation for allowing DMCL to use their parts.

A day later the film crew set up in one of the larger conference rooms in Dunmurry to record the last joint meeting between Lotus and DeLorean staff. It was a watershed event in the contractual relationship between Lotus and DeLorean because it was to witness the handover of the car from the development programme at Hethel to series production at Dunmurry. I was present.

The meeting opened with Barrie Wills enquiring about the completion status of the production bill of materials. The company was six weeks away from producing the first car and we were yet to see a copy of the list of materials with its associated revision levels required to build that production car. Four of us – Harry Steadman, Martin Graham, Colin Pinn (engineering administration manager) and I – had spent the previous three days finalising the latest revision levels with manufacturing and engineering, but only hand-marked versions were available. The question was eventually passed to Mike Loasby, engineering director. In his annoyance at being given what rugby football players call a 'hospital pass' he left the meeting to fetch his copy. (The production bill of materials was finally released on 20 January 1981, the day before the first car was launched. Its first update of many thousands of changes was initiated a few hours later, after the launch of that first car, to accommodate changes to the front suspension assembly.)

This was the last joint DeLorean–Lotus meeting

Chuck attended as managing director of DMCL. A few days later he was invited to New York and was asked to get there quickly, and to travel by Concorde if necessary. On his arrival at Park Avenue he was told that he was being replaced with immediate effect; his replacement, Don Lander, was waiting in the wings, ready to start work. Chuck resigned as managing director on 19 November 1980.

He joked later, when he told me the full story, that 'going to New York by Concorde to get the chop was like going to see Madame Guillotine in a Rolls-Royce'. Even in adversity Chuck could always see the amusing side of life. He was invited to become the new projects director; his new job was to be in Coventry, the office of the production purchasing staff.

In December Lotus Cars presented their proposal for the turbo version of the PRV engine. The offer had a price tag of £3.14 million for development (excluding body tooling) for a twin turbo with a 0–60mph time of 4.9 seconds. Chuck, now in charge of new product development, submitted the proposal to the board. We were also in discussions with Legend Industries to develop a retrofit turbo system available to existing car owners.

Some weeks later there was very little excitement and no formal announcement when the first car built at Dunmurry, pilot car D22, was completed in the first week of December 1980. The small-scale production line in the training building was nearing the end of its useful life as we prepared to move into the new assembly building. The car was not to the definitive specification and was therefore not a saleable product, but nevertheless it was a major milestone in the history of the company.

The DeLorean image was holding up well with the public and the automotive industry, but beneath the surface we still had problems. The experimental bills of materials were out of date within hours of publication. Purchasing staff wrote their own records of the correct and latest version. The master bill of materials document feeding off the IBM computer at Dunmurry was all but useless as it landed in the printer catch tray. Any work instructions were irrelevant as soon as they were drawn and issued, as were service parts instructions.

Although these issues might have given any other company severe concerns as to their viability and sanity, we thought we had made progress. At the end of another difficult year I was looking forward to the Christmas break, knowing that we had made major steps forward. The holiday was scheduled to last from 24 December 1980 to 4 January 1981, or at least that was the plan. I had already been told that the Coventry office had to be open on New Year's Day for support to the factory, although it was conveniently forgotten that this was a national holiday.

In the late evening of 23 December I slipped on the stairs at home and fell, my foot eventually breaking the fall. I realised immediately that this was a serious accident. I had broken five bones in my foot. A knee-length plaster cast was applied at the local accident and emergency department. The cast became a hindrance, and I was now unable to drive or, for that matter, walk with any pace.

On 27 December, while still on Christmas vacation, a secretary from the executive suite in Belfast phoned my home with a message: 'Mr Cafiero wants you in the plant tomorrow.' I informed her that I couldn't travel because of my injury. A few minutes later she called back: 'Mr Cafiero said that tickets would be at Birmingham airport tomorrow morning at 6am for your collection.'

Harry Steadman and Martin Graham had also been summoned, but they lived locally to the plant so their trip was easier. We met the next day at the factory and decided to make use of the time until Gene Cafiero appeared to begin a trek through the new parts status report (a hand-written list of all new purchased parts showing part number, order number and approval status). Line by line, with approximately 900 items to review, with details of sample dates, approval status, recording the details of deliveries to date and revision levels, this clearly was going to take some time. A short while after we'd started Gene entered the room; he was again immaculately dressed. Don Lander was at his side, and they sat quietly in the corner as the three of us ploughed through the parts list. A few minutes into the process and Gene said, 'Hold it!'

He told us that the company only had enough money to last until Easter, 16 weeks away, and if we couldn't produce cars in quantity by that time we were fired. After a knowing exchange of glances with Don he qualified the statement by saying we would be made redundant together with all the other employees as the factory would have to close down due to a shortage of funds. He continued: 'We need two press cars to be flown out to Los Angeles in January and another for the public launch by the third week in January plus four cars to be air-freighted to the US in early February. If you can't do that you're fired because you're incompetent.' He then said 'You can go now' and walked out. Once again, Gene had left the carrot at home.

The three of us lost all interest in the review of the parts list. I caught the midday flight back to England.

Early on New Year's Day as, still hindered by the plaster cast, I couldn't drive, I took the bus to Coventry bus terminus. It was cold and the remnants of snow and slush lay on the ground. I had remained angry with Gene and his comments but was determined that we wouldn't fail, at least with my end of things. I hobbled to the DeLorean offices, blaspheming with every step, vowing that on my demise from this world I would report Gene Cafiero to God at the earliest opportunity.

Exiting from the lift on the fourth floor of Spire House to enter the office area I glanced at the photograph (now housed in the Coventry Car Museum) of the DeLorean car on the wall. It was the first thing to be seen when the lift doors opened. This full-size image was usually inspiring, but that day it failed to make its normal impact. I was alone in the office; it was silent, with no phones or traffic noise; and this was a national holiday.

For the only time during my employment with the company I had lost all interest in the project. The motivation had gone. The positive emotion I'd once enjoyed was disappearing fast and we had yet to produce a car. I doubted if I had the resilience for the challenges that lay ahead. My dreams were falling apart.

The next decision was an easy one. I took myself across the road from the office to the pub and had a few drinks.

The DeLorean marathon was only two years old. What I didn't know then was that we had completed the easy part. The difficult years lay ahead. Happy New Year 1981!

## Chapter 10

# THE FIRST CARS – AND THE SMELL OF SUCCESS

The date set for the start of series production had been 4 January 1981 – and we knew that this was not going to happen. Don Lander, untarnished from any earlier commitments of production timing, would only give a date that was achievable. January for the despatch of the first consignment was now history. The usual suspects came out of the woodwork to pronounce that the original date for production had always been stupid, but of course they'd not been brave enough to impart that information to John DeLorean. Don announced that April 1981 would be the date for the first shipment and this deadline had to be met, no matter what. The change in managing director had bought us a little more time from the government. He explained that we had to perform and to be seen by the world that we were in business.

I was in Belfast for three days that first week of January, then full-time for the next two weeks. The plaster cast on my leg invited some sympathy from the girls in the office but, as might be expected, a great deal of sarcasm from the men. The important thing was that I had now returned to my normal self, full of enthusiasm if not disappointment that cars were not moving off the production line.

The body shop was the most complete of all the manufacturing buildings, with many of the machines and processes now working. Usually they operated to plan, although sometimes the processes took their own direction. At one point in early December the meter reading the resin catalyst levels failed so the operators injected resin into moulds not knowing that the resin would never set. But with hard work, a sense of purpose and determination the multitude of teething problems were overcome, one by one.

The low ambient temperatures experienced in January caused problems for the body shop in their attempt to ramp up production. The VARI tool temperature had to be between 20 and 25°C, quite a challenge in this vast building. Eventually, prior to injecting resin, the moulds were wrapped in huge industrial electric blankets; another success for the DeLorean entrepreneurs.

All that was needed now were stainless steel panels and the whole operation would start to roll.

When in full production all the human senses were awakened on entering the body shop, an immense structure of 191,000 square feet that could hold 70 tennis courts. The smell of styrene from the polyester resin dispensed from the Cellier injection plant was overpowering; the noise of the hand-held panel linishers on the stainless panels masked the noise of the clinch presses mating the inner and outer doors; the sparks of the spot welding machines lit up the areas where the panels were assembled. The whole area was a cacophony of sound and an intensity of light.

There was no doubt that this building was ready for

action, at least for the supply of bodies to the assembly building. They were less prepared than their neighbours for full-scale production.

Most of the early production VARI plastic bodies were despatched to the assembly shop to use as training aids. Body-shop operators used some for practising drilling holes to accommodate plumbing and wiring. A body would require over 200 holes, and at first all the holes were drilled manually. This was a hit-and-miss affair. Drilling the hole in the wrong place would be a disaster as it then had to be filled and redrilled, a time-consuming process. Eventually this process became semi-automated. While some bodies were sent to the training building many others sat outside, to deteriorate as time passed. In total, 500 black cars were made (a black car was either a body shell or a body on a rolling chassis without stainless panels or exterior trim). The downside was that they consumed material and labour, a cost we could ill afford.

Some material was later taken from the black cars to complete early production cars. Other material was supplied from prototype tooling and not to the latest design. Many parts were marked or damaged as they were removed from earlier cars. This would reflect badly on the quality of the first shipment in April.

We had discussions regarding the feasibility of converting the early black bodies to cars and selling them to Japan. The idea was ludicrous, but some management time was spent appraising the suggestion. The scheme probably originated with Roy Nesseth, John's right-hand man, who worked in the shadows of the New York office.

I was tasked with co-ordinating availability of purchased parts for the first car to be completed in late January, an insignificant job given the problems the manufacturing people faced in producing a worthy product for the world to admire from less than perfect parts. After days and nights working non-stop the first car rolled, or more correctly limped, off the assembly line to meet the gaze of the press. I was in Coventry on 21 January when this first car was born. I phoned to ask if anything had fallen off during its short trip around the half-mile test track. If things had gone wrong I was off to South America where Gene couldn't find me...

What I didn't know was that the first car had been driven off the production line earlier in the day and given a quick run around the track – and disaster had struck. The driver hit the kerb and severely damaged the suspension, rendering the car undriveable. Another car was hurriedly brought up to saleroom condition. It was this car that John DeLorean drove out of the factory building into the glare of the camera lights.

The manufacturing people had done a first-class job. This should have been a joyous moment, but the shine had been taken off it by the events that had taken place three weeks earlier, during the Christmas break.

We now had 566 hourly paid employees and 307 non-productive staff working at the factory, soaking up money at an alarming rate. Cars had to be made and shipped by Easter if we were to remain in business. The government demanded that the world and the taxpayer should witness our progress. This was a condition of further government support. Gradually, day by day, production increased. Two cars per day, then three, and in late January the Minister for Economic Affairs advised Parliament in Westminster that by the end of February we'd be producing cars at a rate of 30 per day. We wondered if he was in touch with reality because the numbers mentioned sounded impossible. Schedules for material were issued, cancelled and reissued time and time again, so that the suppliers were not only confused but also becoming concerned about our viability and sanity. At one stage the senior management of Renault complained: 'You can't start and stop our production like a popcorn machine.' But we did and they had no option but to comply.

To get the momentum going and to improve communications a notice was placed at every work station advising how many cars were planned for that day and the number actually produced. As cars passed through the area the notice was updated. Failure to know your department's objectives for the coming days would result in an angry reaction from Don and, for dessert, a bit of venom from Gene. During this period we were forbidden to hold any meeting unless it was about a production-related issue. Any discussion on any matter other than achieving the required daily output was outlawed.

Harry Steadman set up a rework crib in the centre of the assembly building. When parts didn't fit they were hand-modified until the supplier of the part modified the tool and supplied parts to the new specification.

The basic tools used in the crib were a pneumatic router, a hand file and an electric drill. This rework activity commenced with the brackets holding the panels for the front and rear fascias. The assembly operators couldn't fit the part with the single round hole in the bracket so these were modified, as were many other parts, to give some latitude of adjustment by making the fixing holes crucifix shaped. As time passed and more and more items fell into this category the situation had to be sorted quickly. We were receiving up to 20 modifications a day at the start of production, and these demanded a quick turnaround.

Harry Steadman was nominated by George Broomfield as the person in charge of making cars ready for the first shipment, planned for Easter. Harry spent day and night in the EVP (Emissions and Vehicle Preparation) building, directing the completion of cars. He was tirelessly enthusiastic and determined. His pace never faltered as the day continued: he was as lively at eight o'clock in the evening as he'd been a dozen hours earlier. Harry was another man in the right place at the right time for John DeLorean's dream. I have yet to witness his match in any other business.

Progress brought discipline, and this in turn brought procedures. We were now being slowed by the formal quality, engineering and finance procedures we were instructed to follow. The process became painfully slow. We waited for the new drawings to be formally released; we then applied for capital expenditure; once authorised, the supplier would be advised; samples would be obtained; then, following sample approval, bulk supplies were scheduled. A process that had taken two weeks was now estimated to take eight weeks or more. We decided to short-circuit the system: Harry and his colleagues would pass hand-modified drawings to purchasing and we'd get on with the change. The paperwork would follow and allow others to catch up with the process. Slowly we made progress.

Each evening a review was held in Don Lander's office, reflecting on the day's output. Gene Cafiero usually attended, with Barrie Wills and George Broomfield ready to give the answers. Harry Steadman, Martin Graham and myself often attended.

Failure to meet the required output was analysed in detail. Availability of material was often an issue, as suppliers second-guessed our requirements. Who could blame them, given our constant changes? The meeting usually lasted an hour but it was always intense and seemed longer.

The company's business plan was based upon the assumption that a car would take 50 man-hours to complete. For the first three months of production each car took 500 hours to make. The cost of the black cars manufactured in late 1980 and January 1981 added to our financial problems as most of the cost of the materials and labour was non-recoverable. These costs were eating away at the financial pot. We needed additional money urgently.

About this time we learned details of John's discussions with Chrysler. The news originated from the 'Chrysler Mafia' network in Belfast. The US government had agreed to support Chrysler's core car division in the US, but not the peripheral activities of marine and other non-car activities; they could arrange their own bail-out. We heard that John had been discussing swapping the Belfast car company for the marine division of Chrysler, his interest in boats rekindled from his time at Chris-Craft. Given our commitment to the DeLorean programme and the effort we had already made to support the man and the company, the news was a huge disappointment. Perhaps the story was untrue, but we just didn't know. We hoped that the rumours were unfounded. We heard nothing more of the negotiations so the deal must have fallen through, if there'd been one under discussion at all. Chrysler Marine was eventually sold in 1984; Chrysler Defense was sold to General Dynamics in 1982; Chrysler Cars UK was sold to Peugeot.

John DeLorean was now considering the future for his own engineering activities, and he had plans to occupy the now-vacant Grundig factory only a few yards from the DeLorean perimeter fence. This was to be a centre of excellence for DeLorean engineering and the new home for purchasing staff, who would be relocated from Coventry. A test track was to be established some ten miles from the plant. None of these plans came to anything, however, as we were continually running short of cash. Although the master plan was completed it lay in the filing cabinet, waiting for the day that we had surplus funds – which of course we never had.

John DeLorean was back with his begging bowl, this time asking for a government loan of £10 million. On 2 February 1981 the Northern Ireland Secretary, Humphrey Atkins, told the Cabinet: 'To let this project go now would be seen, particularly by the minority community, as betrayal in the one area, economic development, where the government could act positively. It would no doubt be contrasted with our continuing support for the largely Protestant Harland and Wolff and unhappy comparisons would certainly be drawn with our current support of BL [British Leyland].'

In a letter to the Prime Minister dated 3 February 1981, Mr Atkins added: 'I am convinced that for reasons mainly special to Northern Ireland we should accede to this request.'

We were given a £10 million loan on 12 February 1981; Adam Butler, Minister for Economic Development in Northern Ireland, announced the decision in the House of Commons. The debate in Parliament afterwards bordered on the bitter. Adam Butler thought he had finished for the day when he said: 'No more selective assistance would be given to the DMC12 project. The company is well aware of that.' But the vitriolic exchange continued for some time afterwards. Jock Bruce-Gardyne called John DeLorean a con man, an unusual comment in the House of Commons where MPs are careful not to abuse their privilege of being immune from civil action for slander while performing their duties.

Day by day we made progress, but by the end of February we were still only making 12 cars a day as against the 30 promised by the Minister for Economic Affairs. Don Lander called a meeting to review the status of activity. At one point, one of the manufacturing staff raised a quality concern over an electrical part which he had brought with him as a 'show and tell' part of the meeting. It was the inertia switch, which gave so much trouble over the life of the car. Don asked one senior manager present to identify the part. When the recipient of the question declared that he didn't know Don threw the part at him and hit him mid-chest, saying 'Find out!' This was one of two occasions I saw Don Lander red-faced with rage.

There were many other quality problems and concerns – parts didn't fit, particularly the exterior panels, doors, front and rear fascias, rear louvres and engine covers and, worst of all, there were water leaks through the doors. The doors didn't latch correctly, the rear louvre was cracking in several places, interior trim was also looking messy and the A-post trim structure was far from being complete.

Regardless of all these problems, the car was officially launched at Europe's prestigious Geneva International Motor Show on 5 March 1981. Geneva has been the launch site for new cars and concept cars since 1905, giving the general public the first opportunity to see these vehicles. The DeLorean car was different because it had been in the news many times already and the styling was well known – but it still attracted significant attention. Its eccentric brand of stainless steel and gull wing doors stole the show from the multinational brands displaying their new babies for the first time.

The final formal commercial and technical meeting between Renault and DMCL was planned for the next day in Geneva. It was to take place in the Hôtel du Rhône. I'd arrived the night before. John DeLorean and other senior board members were staying at the President Wilson hotel. By this time Dick Brown, who had done so much for the car company, had been thrown off the main board, which now consisted of 16 people. One of the new appointees was Cristina DeLorean. Many of the other names were new to me and were not from the automotive business, being mostly lawyers or accountants.

At this time the US operations employed 55 staff in New York; Dunmurry had 1,335 members of staff, of which 1,000 were operatives in the factory.

On 16 March we received the certificate of conformity from the EPA and the stricter Californian emissions (CARB) one appeared on 31 March 1981.

A few weeks later Chuck kicked off the European development programme to allow the sale of the car in the UK and the wider European Community. The change from a standard US car to European specifications involved a considerable amount of cost and engineering work. As we didn't have the time or resources at Dunmurry to undertake this activity, the complete package was outsourced to Wooler Hodec Ltd in England. They were contracted to convert 28 cars supplied from Dunmurry. The cars were unsaleable structures taken from the early batch of vehicles built at the start of the year. Metal and soft trim parts were to be fabricated using Wooler Hodec's own resources. Others parts required the input of either DMCL purchasing or engineering.

The programme was superbly organised by Stuart Craven who worked for purchasing in Coventry. The plan was to complete this trial to assess viability and cost, then use these first cars as replacements for Ford lease cars currently on the DeLorean fleet in Dunmurry. If the financial numbers stacked up we were to build more right-hand-drive cars at Dunmurry. We didn't get that far in the programme, however, and no right-hand-drive cars were made in Ireland.

The first bulk shipment to the USA went to plan – or at least the timing was on schedule, if not the quality of the product. It was Easter weekend. The car cargo ship *Continental Highway* arrived at Belfast docks on Saturday 18 April. The 379 cars were ferried from the plant, six at a time, on car transporters contracted with Northern Ireland Carriers (NIC), travelling through the Dunmurry gates to Stormont wharf where they were loaded on to the ship. It sailed on Easter Sunday, 19 April; its destination was Long Beach, California. Television crews and newspaper reporters were there in abundance, as were employees and their families. It was a wonderful sunny day and we all had great hopes for the future.

The following week Gene Cafiero invited DMCL employees to a briefing in the assembly building. He was usually the epitome of sartorial elegance, his suits of the finest quality, his shoes shining, hair immaculate, with not a crease to be witnessed anywhere on his clothes or his face. This day was different. He was standing on a podium, coatless, his shirtsleeves rolled up as if ready for action. He started by briefly thanking everyone for their efforts, and then continued speaking for 20 minutes or so, telling the assembled throng how important it was to get things right first time. During his speech I was certain that he was looking at me, only me and no one else but me. He rounded off his monologue with the immortal words that will live with me forever more: 'You ain't seen nothing yet.'

How true. How very true.

## Chapter 11

# THE IRA HUNGER STRIKES

The euphoria that buzzed about the factory following the Easter Sunday shipment didn't last long. Two weeks after the ship sailed from Belfast harbour the first hunger striker died. Bobby Sands had been an inmate at the Maze prison, ten miles south-west of Belfast. He was the first of ten IRA hunger strikers to die over the next five months.

The hunger strikes were a protest against the withdrawal of de facto prisoner of war status, which provided paramilitary prisoners with privileges similar to those granted to POWs, as specified in the Geneva Convention. Under this covenant inmates were allowed to wear their own clothes and were not forced to perform prison work. They were also allowed free association within their paramilitary factions in the notorious H block section of the Maze prison. A change of policy by the British government removed these privileges.

Bobby Sands was the first prisoner to refuse nourishment, beginning his hunger strike on 1 March 1981. It was only a matter of time: his death occurred 66 days later during the early hours of 5 May 1981. He was 27 years of age and the Member of Parliament for Fermanagh and South Tyrone, although he was never to take his seat in the House of Commons, nor had there been any intention that he would do so. His election, occurring while he was in prison, was a publicity and public relations coup for the IRA, suggesting to the wider world that the majority of Bobby Sands's constituents supported the Republican movement; it also, however, led to a widespread misconception that most people in Northern Ireland held the same opinion.

Minutes after Bobby Sands's death was announced the sound of dustbin lids rattling against the ground slowly gathered pace throughout the Catholic community. The noise made its way from Twinbrook, where the news was first heard, three miles onwards to Belfast city centre where it reached its crescendo. People in Nationalist areas flooded on to the streets in the early hours, some to pay their respects or pray, others to create disorder. Those living in central Belfast heard the noise of the violent clashes between Republican sympathisers and the British army throughout the night.

Shortly after the news broke a car hijacked in the Twinbrook housing estate was driven towards the flimsy outer gates of the DeLorean factory. The gates gave way easily, allowing the protesters to move forwards to the inner gate. This proved more troublesome for the rioters as this gate was designed to hold firm even under extreme force. This inner gate was only a few feet from the Portakabin huts erected in early 1979 and temporarily occupied by staff until the offices in the manufacturing areas were completed. A little further from the Portakabin was the training building, just out of throwing range of a Molotov cocktail. Several petrol bombs were thrown at the Portakabin huts, however, the resulting fire spreading rapidly through the wooden structures and burning it to the ground.

One of the first acts of reactive violence to Bobby Sands's death occurred a few hours later when a Protestant delivery milkman and his 14-year-old son, who happened to be in the wrong place at the wrong time, were stoned to death by protesters. The three deaths made the headlines on every international television and radio station. By early morning every household in Northern Ireland had heard the news about Bobby Sands and the barbaric stoning of the milkman and his schoolboy son.

Some DeLorean employees who lived in Twinbrook feared further violence on the streets and the mass involvement of the army. They didn't make it to the factory that day, or if they did they waited until later to see how events were unfolding. About one-third of the workforce failed to show up for work.

Later that morning the parish priest of St Luke's, the Catholic church located half a mile from the factory, arrived at the DeLorean offices to emphasise to the management that the fire was the work of hot-headed youths and was certainly not endorsed by the wider Twinbrook community. He stressed that the local population appreciated the factory's presence and were grateful for the employment and hope that it gave to the people of West Belfast. The priest was in the training building reception area when I arrived for work that day.

John DeLorean first heard the news of the fire on the radio early morning New York time. Eager to know the extent of the damage he summoned Shaun Harte, then in New York, to advise him of the impact the fire would have on production and to report on the extent of the fire damage. After a few calls to Belfast Shaun was able to tell him that very little disruption would occur because the occupants of the Portakabin huts were ready to move to the main assembly building some time over the next ten days. All personnel records had been lost but could be replaced, as could the drawings of production material. Copies of the drawings were kept at the DeLorean Coventry office and the originals were at Lotus Cars, filed away for product liability reasons.

Bobby Sands's body was taken from the Maze to the family home in Twinbrook where his mother and sister lived, their house just a few hundred yards from the DeLorean factory gate. On Wednesday evening his remains were taken to St Luke's, the coffin accompanied by over 50,000 people walking in silence to the church in heavy rain. On the day of the funeral, after a requiem mass, the cortege walked to the Republican plot in Milltown cemetery three miles away. A total of 100,000 people congregated there, many travelling from the far corners of Ireland.

One of the banners carried by the crowd bore the title 'DeLorean Nationalist Workers', with a DeLorean car smashing through the letter H (for H block). This infuriated John DeLorean when he watched the scenes on television. It angered him more than the burning of the Portakabin huts, or any other event, because his own image was being tarnished.

The day after the fire the managing director of DMCL, Don Lander, wrote to Kenneth Bloomfield,

Permanent Secretary to the Department of Economic Development. His letter stated that:

'The fire had badly damaged the confidence of potential investors and [that] further funding would be difficult from normal financial institutions. Further, suppliers would now reduce their exposure in the project and withdraw the favourable credit terms that had been negotiated early in the programme.'

Subsequently the company would require extensions to the existing loans and further bridging finance of £11 million. This was in addition to the £7 million claimed by DeLorean for damages to property and consequential loss caused by the firebombing. This last claim was a massive exaggeration. Even the £425,327 that was paid out could be regarded as excessive. However, the government relented and in early summer a further guaranteed bank loan of £10 million was agreed. This would expire on 31 December 1981, a key date in the history of the company.

There were other prisoners on hunger strike at the Maze prison, men preparing for death. Disruption of production at the factory would occur regularly due to absenteeism by those attending the wakes and funerals, or employees fearing to travel to work.

A week after Bobby Sands's death Don Lander called a meeting to discuss contingency actions to resolve the problems caused by the high absenteeism and to review future volumes of production. The large oval table in the meeting room that could seat 18 had just ten seats filled. Don sat to one side at the top of the table. The chair next to him was vacant, waiting for Myron Stylianides, the personnel director of DMCL, to arrive and make an announcement. While we waited for him Don explained that, however uncomfortable we were with the events that had occurred during the previous week, it was imperative that we maintained output. We had to plan around the events that were unfolding at the Maze and the resultant disruption to production that would inevitably occur. The government had to witness our ongoing progress in ramping up production. Excuses, however valid, would not be tolerated.

It was Myron's task to liaise with the police and the army to estimate when the next hunger striker would die, and the one after that, and so on. We were told not to take notes as the meeting would be strictly confidential – except, of course, that we had to communicate the inevitable revision to schedules to the supply base. How we were to do that in detail without giving reasons was not explained.

The idea of planning production of a car around the death of a person was abhorrent to most of us in the room. It is said that in times of extreme anxiety the mind attempts to disguise repugnant events so as to lessen the burden on the soul. One such event took place for me that day in May 1981.

Myron entered the room to give us an update of what he had just learned after his briefing from the military. He appeared exhausted, breathless and at the point of collapse, sweat on his brow, clearly nervous, his speech hesitant. As Myron was of Greek origin my mental image was of him as the legendary athlete who ran from Marathon to Athens, a distance of 26 miles, to deliver the news of the defeat of the Persians. Having completed his mission, the messenger subsequently dropped dead. However, Myron simply reported, one by one, the estimated dates of death for each hunger striker – Francis Hughes, Patsy O'Hara, Raymond McCreesh – the names tolling on until I mentally turned off the sound.

The first area to be hit in the event of a shortage of staff would be the body shop, which had a predominance of Catholic operatives, many of whom lived on the Twinbrook housing estate. One of the actions to be taken from the meeting was to increase the stock of black VARI bodies ready for onward shipment to the assembly building. Harry Steadman recalls that the instruction was to fill the area allocated for body stock to the maximum and to have more bodies available on free-standing trolleys if production stopped. Every space in the body shop was to be filled with completed moulded bodies; the overflow would be stored in the assembly area.

A week after Bobby Sands's funeral, in the early evening, I heard the clatter of dustbin lids crashing against kerbstones. The noise was coming from the Twinbrook housing estate, only two or three hundred yards away, and it was a sound that signalled death. It increased in strength, becoming louder and louder as the minutes passed. Another hunger striker had died. Who had been the next man on Myron's list? I gave some thought to what Myron had said that morning in the conference room – then I thought about the changes to the production schedule at the factory –

then it was back to the man who had died – then the suppliers' schedules and what would happen next. I didn't know what to think. I was here to help build a car and a factory, and this just wasn't in my plan.

Later that night there was more trouble at the Twinbrook gate and another claim for damages was to be submitted to the authorities by DMCL. Francis Hughes was buried three days later, on 15 May. Over the next five months another eight hunger strikers would die.

The directors were now content to leave the management team alone to control the problem and delegate the detail to the appropriate line managers and supervisors. There were no further meetings to discuss the issue, but every time a hunger striker died all those who had sympathy for the deceased and the cause would line up in the body shop and bow their heads in silence. They would then return to work, the whole process taking less than 20 minutes.

On the day of the funerals many workers from Twinbrook didn't show up for work, and the exit roads from the estate would be manned by small groups of Republican supporters, stopping cars and pedestrians to suggest that they might wish to attend the funeral rather than go to the factory. Most if not all of those stopped by the stewards returned to their homes. Some changed clothes to more casual weekend wear and tried their luck again later in the day, saying that they were going out to get milk or bread. In this way some eventually arrived for work, albeit rather late.

Two or three evenings a week a demonstration would take place outside the inner gates. It was usually the same well-known Republican with a megaphone to carry the message the 300 yards to the manufacturing area, calling for all Nationalists to down tools and strike. In May 1981, in the early evening, only the body-shop workers were in the plant. Occasionally a few of the more hot-blooded elements involved with the demonstration would toss a stone or other missiles. It is a matter of record that the factory had ten firebomb attacks over a seven-week period between May and June 1981.

Early one evening in late May the usual protesters were making themselves known at the inner gate. The noise made by the rattling of dustbin lids against the security gate became monotonous and irritating. I decided to leave my foxhole, the broom cupboard, to visit the assembly building to take a break and a short walk. As I approached the rear of the huge assembly building I heard the sound of diesel engines in the area between there and the emissions block. Around the corner I could see around 20 army troop carriers, each one with the capacity to hold ten soldiers. The soldiers had disembarked from the trucks; they were hidden from the protesters' view by the assembly building. There were over 200 soldiers lining up for orders, all in full riot gear and complete with SLR rifles, ready to take their positions throughout the factory.

Returning to the training building, close to the Twinbrook gate, I could see that soldiers had already occupied the first and second floors, lying flat on the walkways between the desks. I walked the 30 or so paces to the end of the building, zigzagging to avoid a soldier or his rifle. There were more soldiers on the stairs and landing leading to the reception area. On the top floor, lying prostrate, were two soldiers in the ante-room between Shaun Harte's and Barrie Wills's offices. The demonstrators at the gate had no way of knowing that the army was only a few feet away. Trouble was brewing. The army was present in force; the BBC were setting up a camera position on a small tor next to the gate, well behind the demonstrators, ready to catch the action. These were the ingredients for a full-scale riot.

The scene that only I could witness was surreal. Beneath my feet, lying flat on the floor, were several soldiers with faces blacked out, dressed in full riot gear, with rifles at their sides. Thirty feet further away but outside were the demonstrators at the inner security gate. Twenty feet further on were the TV cameras.

The phone rang at the secretary's desk in the ante-room just a few feet away. In order to answer it I placed one leg over a soldier's head on the floor and stuck out the other, stork-like in the air, my head resting on the windowpane to retain my balance. A voice said, 'Hello Nick, it's your mother.' She was calling from her home in England, where she was watching live television shots of the factory and could see the protesters at the DeLorean gate. I told her that I was a long way from the events she could see on television. I lied.

I went to Barrie's office to suggest to him that it might be wise to vacate the building. My urgent appeal, relayed to him via nervous body language, nodding my head towards the factory gate to his rear, was ignored. He was in full blast on the phone to a delinquent supplier and didn't need my posturing as a distraction. He gestured with his hands for me to sit. But sitting was not something I wanted to do; the word 'running' came more immediately to mind. After a few minutes, and much to Barrie's annoyance, we were asked by one of the army officers orchestrating the security operation to leave the building. Barrie was upset at being given orders, but on this rare occasion he did as he was told.

We exited the factory that evening through the Seymour Hill gate. As we reached the main street we saw two young girls, hand in hand, dressed in Brownie uniforms. They had a skip in their step and were clearly excited about going to their weekly meeting. What a contrast to events less than half a mile away, where a mini-riot was about to start. There in front of us was a scene that could have been taken from any peaceful country in the world.

The soldiers made frequent invited trips to the factory during the summer and continued clandestine visits to the factory until October 1981, when the hunger strikes were called off. The world's press were losing interest in the hunger strike story. Sacrifices had been made but there seemed little point in continuing.

But only then did the soldiers stop coming to the plant – and I stopped lying to my mother.

*Chapter 12*

# STAFF EXPANSION AND THE VISIT OF A LEGEND

F rom January to the end of May 1981 we employed
 a further 434 hourly paid workers and yet more
office staff. Moving location from the training building
to the main factory gave us more space to house these
latest recruits. There was room for even more and they
arrived, month after month, often without justification
or need.

It was John DeLorean's intention to employ over 2,000
people by the end of the year. The master agreement,
signed in July 1978, had given him until the end of
the fifth year to achieve this objective but it was to his
advantage to meet the obligation earlier. Employing
2,000 workers allowed the company to convert loans to
grants that were by definition not repayable. To fund this
switch, the Belfast company was awarded a generous
employment allowance of £6,500 per employee, hence
the rush to get people on board.

In the last week of May the first shipment of cars,
despatched on Easter Sunday from Belfast, arrived at
Long Beach, California. From here they travelled by
car transporter to the DeLorean quality centre at Santa
Ana, to be inspected and reworked to a merchantable
quality. The quality control activities were publicly

described as the repair of transportation damage, road testing, safety checks, cleaning, polishing and pre-delivery inspection, but the quality centre was to encompass much more than that initially planned or expected. The 20,000 square foot building was eventually crammed with operatives working a 12-hour day, seven days a week. The costs were estimated to be up to $2,000 per car. This was in addition to the $325 shipping costs.

Dick Brown was expecting some element of reworking, but not to the degree that he witnessed when the cars arrived. Water had leaked into the cars, so both inner and outer seals needed to be refitted or replaced. The rear pontoons also contained significant amounts of water and had to be drained. The interior door A-posts were a mess, with excess trim hanging over the screen trim. Wiring harnesses were hanging loose at the driver's knees; this not only looked bad but was also dangerous. The batteries on most of the cars were dead, making movement of the vehicles a nightmare. Another electrical problem concerned the Ducellier alternator fitted by Renault; at 75amps this was under-rated for the peak power load required, and it was exchanged for a Motorola 90amp to overcome the problem.

Despite all these problems, however, in early June we learned that shares were to be issued for DMC (the DMCL holding company) – the company was to be floated on the stock market. The public stock offering was arranged by Bache Halsey Stuart Shields, the underwriting and brokerage firm. A 100-page prospectus outlined the profile of the company, including details of the balance sheet and finances (which, of course, failed to detail the GPD money).

The flotation might have been a surprise to the workforce, but not to the UK government. The master agreement included a clause that allowed John DeLorean to buy out the UK government and other shareholders, in whole or in part, within four years from the start of production. This included the buyout of DeLorean Research Partnership. (DLRP were to become notable as the main commercial body alleged to have been defrauded in the GPD deal.)

In the event of a successful flotation John DeLorean would receive most of the money, as his rearrangement of the management stock options earlier in the year had ensured that this would be the case. All stock options offered to the directors of the company in their original contracts of employment would become worthless once the new offering was released. At the start of discussions regarding the flotation there were some heated exchanges between John DeLorean and NIDA. John objected to a clause regarding the timescale in which he could dispose of his shares. NIDA wanted an extended period. DeLorean objected.

To promote the share issue we received instructions to double production to 80 cars per day. Naturally, a higher output and associated sales and profit would make the stock prospectus look more attractive.

The personnel department advertised for more workers in the local newspapers. We estimated that a further 1,000 people were required to meet the increased output. To satisfy the demand, the purchasing and materials departments were to ensure that sufficient manufacturing capacity existed in the supply base and to issue material schedules to reflect the increased requirement. The earliest date we judged as being feasible for the higher daily rate was September, just three months away.

Because the car was well received (at least that was our perception) and sales were going well (again, our perception), we regarded this increased output as a wonderful opportunity for the company, the staff and the local community. To add to our credibility, the first royalty payment of £205,350 was made to the government on 30 June; by this time we had shipped 1,110 cars. Things seemed to be going well.

Actually, the opposite was true. Coming events would result in the financial elastic band snapping towards the end of the year, to be followed by receivership, and then the ultimate closure of the company a year later.

Further bad news arrived on 8 July. Joe McDonnell, from the Lenadoon housing estate in West Belfast, became the fifth hunger striker to die.

Although we closed for our annual two-week vacation on 10 July, work continued for many. Staff in the despatch department at Dunmurry were busy preparing for the departure of a further 525 cars on 17 July. Meanwhile, in California, while Dick Brown was publicly ecstatic at the arrival of his new car, declaring in a press statement that 'IT'S A WINNER', he was privately furious that the cars were despatched in such poor condition. Key workers from Dunmurry, including operators, electricians and supervisors, were flown to California on Sunday 12 July to assist in the quality centre and to offer their experience of the assembly processes. The intention of the visit was twofold: first, to assist in the quality centre, and second, on their return to advise the factory of the problems encountered by Dick Brown's team.

Later in July Zora Arkus-Duntov, whose work on the Chevrolet Corvette earned him the title 'father of the Corvette', arrived at Dunmurry. This was one of several visits he made to the factory. It was a great tonic for the employees and seemingly yet a further sign that we had a great future. I was introduced to him in the coffee room in the training building. His stories about life at General Motors were received in silence and with respect – this man was a legend in the automotive business. He talked warmly about our car and John DeLorean, his speech interrupted only by a frequent puff of a cigarette or the chance to light another. He'd been hired as a consultant to the company some years earlier and had evaluated the first DeLorean prototypes. His visit to Dunmurry was to discuss the position of chief engineer. He later declined John Delorean's offer but was retained as a consultant.

In July we were producing an average of 35 cars a day and plans for the ramp-up to 80 cars a day were making progress, but there were a few hitches. Many didn't come to light until the system and the suppliers were tested to the limit. The suppliers were naturally hesitant to commit to more stock and work in progress, given the false starts earlier in the year.

One major problem popped up in early August. The supplier of the cast road wheels advised that they had found a major problem with the casting process of the rear wheel. A cold shut had been identified in the manufacturing process. This occurs when molten metal slows as it progresses through the mould and in the process cools. The flow then meets the metal flowing in the opposite direction, with the two streams of metal meeting but not welding. The result is a definite line, similar to a crack, and is a weak spot. As we had not received any reports of failure in the field it was decided that cars in service would not be recalled.

The ten sets of tools involved were taken out of commission and modified. The wheel design was changed to allow greater flow of material through the casting. This meant a physical change to the style of the wheel. Week by week the tools were changed without interrupting supply. Many cars had two different styles of rear wheel either side of the vehicle, but as the owner couldn't see both at the same time it was reckoned that it didn't matter and they would never notice. At first no one did...

*Chapter 13*

# LIFE IN THE FACTORY AND THE DARKER SIDE OF BELFAST

*'*To live the dream' was a phrase coined by the DeLorean marketing team, but it could equally have applied to those seeking work in the new high tech DeLorean factory in Dunmurry. Who was this man, John DeLorean, arriving like manna from heaven in an area of high unemployment where to dream was the territory of the unwise? His film-star looks, his beautiful wife and a car from the next century all seemed too good to be true. All this was coming to Dunmurry. Who could believe it?

By the time of the groundbreaking ceremony in October 1978 800 people had applied for jobs at the factory. Many were unemployed; others that were in employment were ready to leave their current job to work for John DeLorean. This venture was too good an opportunity to miss. Some applicants wrote to John DeLorean in New York, others to the site in Dunmurry, while many contacted the Department of Commerce in Belfast. After they'd completed the application form, and if they looked suitable, an interview was next. If they were lucky they would get the offer of a job.

At the start of their employment each new employee was supplied with a brochure which outlined the

DeLorean programme. This included details of the size of the site, the individual buildings and their purpose, information about the car, including how it was to be constructed, and specifications of the PRV engine and Renault gearbox.

Terms and conditions of employment were explained, as were the company's policies on sectarian images and religious tolerance within the workplace. Some of the larger manufacturing concerns in Belfast allowed national flags, sectarian football shirts, religious images and other provocative material to be shown or worn in the workplace, but the DeLorean management insisted that these things had no place in their factory. Any clothing that could be regarded as confrontational was banned, as were Catholic images or photographs of the Pope and the Holy Cross, or equivalent Protestant images or clothing, or pictures of the Queen. No calendars or posters of any sort adorned the offices or the factory walls; only material supplied by the company was permitted. Any default was dealt with immediately and effectively.

One local woman accepted for employment after her initial interview was Bridie Johnston. She worked on the engine dress line in the assembly area; her shift started at 6am. She was out of bed before five o'clock to allow time to prepare the day ahead for herself and her youngest child. It was a short walk of a few hundred yards to the factory from her house in Twinbrook, just across the road from the DeLorean plant. Bridie was one of the thousand employees that started work in midsummer 1981 to meet the manufacturing schedule of 80 cars a day. Her job was to attach the engine harnesses and fuel pipes to the PRV engine. Bridie worked hard and during the time she was employed by DMCL, like many others, she didn't take any sick leave. She couldn't afford to lose this job. There were very few about during the recession and certainly none that paid this well and with the excellent working conditions that the DeLorean plant offered. At 50 she felt lucky to be given the position. Bridie was used to hard work: her first job had been in the weaving mills of Belfast, starting at 14 years of age.

Joe Murray (clock number 1065) was employed at DeLorean as a maintenance craftsman; his pay was £90 per week with plenty of overtime available. Joe worked the standard shift, from 8am to 4.30pm, with 30 minutes for lunch. At break times he could chose between the rest areas in the assembly area and the canteen located close to the employee gates in a large Portakabin. Joe recalls that the company provided overalls for every worker on the production line. Clean overalls were placed in each employee's locker every weekend by Waveney Laundry, who took away the dirty set to clean, press and make available for the following week.

Geraldine Maxwell worked for Grundig, the tape recorder company, for six years before it closed following the murder of its managing director, Thomas Niedermayer. The factory was located 100 yards from the DeLorean site on the Dunmurry Industrial Estate. Following her redundancy from Grundig Geraldine worked on the assembly line at DeLorean, installing air conditioning units into cars. Her shifts rotated; first an early start at 6am working to 2pm, two weeks later changing to the afternoon shift from 2pm to 10pm. She commenced employment in the summer of 1981 with the ramp-up to 80 cars a day.

Neal Barclay resigned from his job at Enkalon in Antrim to start work at DeLorean. His employment commenced on 16 March 1981 in the vehicle shipping department. He proclaims to this day, as many do, that this was the best job of his life. He was one of thousands living the dream.

Ernie Benson, who worked in the personnel department, recalls one young man who applied for a job; the applicant lived on the Ballymurphy estate in West Belfast. The unemployment rate in this area was up to 50%. For those that didn't claim unemployment benefit, many more claimed invalidity living allowance. Ernie remembers the interview with the young man. He was eager to work and excited about the new DeLorean venture. At 26 years of age he was married with six children but he'd not worked since leaving school. Ernie asked why he wanted to work, because his state benefits would be more than the DeLorean job could offer. He replied: 'I want to work because very few men work where I live. It would be good for me and my pride and to show my children that their father has a job, particularly at the DeLorean factory.' He started his first job a few weeks later. His dream lasted just seven months before the first redundancies hit.

A second production shift started in the summer of 1981, with the assembly area working 6am to 2pm, and 2pm to 10pm for the second shift. The body shop worked a 24-hour shift pattern. The weekend was reserved for VARI body tool maintenance.

At the start of the production programme modifications came quickly and often. There were a few local manufacturers who supplied material to the plant. One particular supplier was located about a mile from DMCL, and on one occasion a drawing had to be taken to him quickly. I asked if the drawing, which I placed in a large envelope, could be delivered by the quickest possible method – and a member of the material control team offered to deliver the package after work. This was in early 1981, with army roadblocks on most main roads searching vehicles and looking out for any unusual activity.

It was dark. Surely no one would pay attention to the volunteer postman parking his car adjacent to the front door of the company, folding the envelope and putting it through the letterbox? But this was a restricted area and leaving a car unattended in such a controlled zone, for however short a time, was strictly forbidden. 'I only left the car for a few seconds,' he told us later.

The good news was that we received the modified parts the next day. The bad news was that that British army had noticed a person running away from a building, having pushed a suspect device through a letterbox. He was thrown into the rear of an army vehicle and asked for his identity and address. Further complications followed because he lived in Catholic West Belfast and the envelope was posted through a letterbox in Protestant South Belfast. Clearly, then, because of his address and the manner of his 'crime' he was a terrorist by association. Unable to prove the contents of the envelope, he was put in jail until the supplier could confirm that the suspected letter bomb was no more than a drawing and a note from me. Much to his credit, the man worked all the next day at DeLorean, despite having had little sleep. He enjoyed a few free beers for a short time, until the next casualty had a tale to tell.

This story is typical of many events that occurred in Northern Ireland during the Troubles. People in Northern Ireland still mask the obscene events that happened with humour. Most stories told about that era are similar. Who would want to talk about the threats, the bombs and murders that most people experienced in their community, and if they did, who would listen? But everyone likes a funny story. It was the spirit and determination of this man, and many more like him, that built the factory at Dunmurry.

Generally my own experiences outside work were mundane. Of course one was extra careful, because if there was one nationality not welcome in parts of West Belfast it was the English. Born in Birmingham, it was difficult to hide my English accent and on occasion being in the wrong place brought its problems.

One evening, shortly after production had started at the plant, and having failed to get into the Conway (used by DeLorean staff as the hotel of choice), I checked into a hotel which was located further into West Belfast. As I sat in one of the wing-backed leather chairs in the lounge bar of the hotel, reading the *Financial Times* (as everyone does, of course, in West Belfast), wearing my nicely pressed pinstripe suit, my head was deep in the paper. A wedding, which I was later to learn was a Republican event, was in full swing in the ballroom next door.

Suddenly a drunk, a guest from the wedding, staggered past me and, having noticed I was alone, sat down and started to talk. Initially this was a one-way conversation, with my unwelcome visitor doing the talking, or more accurately the slurring. Then he noticed my English accent and said, 'Are you a Brit?'

The word 'Brit' is a term used in Belfast to describe a soldier. In my naivety I confirmed that I was indeed a Brit, as in my part of the world the word describes any Englishman living overseas. This one comment was to get me into a spot of bother.

The man announced loudly (and drunkenly) to his friends: 'This is a friend of mine, a Brit at that.' He enquired whether I'd ever worked at the Castlereagh Police Interrogation Centre, and then told me: 'I was there once.'

Clearly he had been there on a number of occasions. I hoped that, at some point, he might wish to talk about football or some other sport instead, but his voice merely increased in volume as he pursued his line of questioning. His wife came over and told him to get away from me and proceeded to pour a glass of beer over his head as an inducement for him to move.

Another man came over and the drunk said, 'He's a big 'en in the RAH [IRA], this one' – information that I was not pleased to hear. The new participant in our conversation was sober and asked a number of questions. In 30 seconds I'd told him all I knew about the British motor industry over the last hundred years. His suggestion was that I might wish to pack and leave the hotel immediately, as he couldn't vouch for the actions of some of his less sober colleagues. In my mind's eye they had already thrown the rope over the tree and gone to get the horse on which to sit me. I left the hotel forthwith.

From this experience I learned that speaking with an English accent in West Belfast was perhaps not a good idea, and that it might be best to keep a low profile in any pubs or hotels that I might frequent. The flaw, of course, is that, as every gentleman will know, when nature calls everyone on earth starts to chat to his neighbour at the urinal. 'Good craic tonight, eh?' 'Weather's bad, isn't it?' An answer is a must. Any answer. How could this be done without betraying my English accent? The solution I developed was a stammer: I'd speak with the hesitation and repetition of a Tommy gun... 'err, err, err, I'm, I'm, I'm' – and very soon the questioner would disappear hurriedly. It worked time after time.

As though we didn't have enough problems at the factory, things were made worse by numerous bomb scares during the summer months of 1981. These resulted in the entire factory being evacuated every time, and the premises searched to locate the suspect device – 72 acres of land and 14 acres of buildings. The whole process could take up to an hour to complete. The workforce from the training building, assembly area, body shop, maintenance and EVP buildings were evacuated to the grassy banks of the Seymour Hill entrance outside the factory gate. With the search complete, the 'all clear' was announced by the personnel director, Myron, using a megaphone to invite everyone back to work. His announcement often had to be repeated more than once, particularly for those with hearing difficulties – and that appeared to be most of the workforce, who were now quite relaxed, basking in the summer sunshine.

Daytime threats were rare; most hoax calls came at night and especially in the early hours. Research by DeLorean security staff and police revealed that the night-time bomb threats were made from inside the DeLorean factory complex, specifically in the main assembly area, that building becoming vacant after 10pm when the last shift finished work there. All phones in the factory's public areas were usually programmed for internal use only – except for one in the assembly shop which was permanently connected, by mistake, to the outside world. This was the phone used by the caller. It was mounted on a support stanchion in the storage area in the assembly building. The assembly building covered six acres and included production lines and material storage areas with wide aisles to allow forklift truck access. It was the next building to the body shop. The assembly building area was lit by emergency lighting after 10pm.

The calls usually came at the same time, about 4am, a few hours before the night shift in the body shop was due to finish. A call two hours before the end of the shift would result in an early finish; it was pointless trying to get work restarted afterwards. The employees were paid for their time – after all, it wasn't their fault if they had to finish early.

A plan was made to catch the culprit. This had to be undertaken in complete secrecy, and it was only later that I learned the details.

One night, just after the assembly shift finished at 10pm, security staff set themselves up in a large crate, similar to a hide used by bird watchers. They had a good view of the phone in question via a flap in the crate.

The box was not out of place as the area was used for material storage and large boxes of many kinds were usual in this location. The security staff, complete with torches, thermos flasks and small seats, sat quietly in the crate in a state of nervous expectation, waiting for the bomb hoaxer to make his call.

First on the scene in the early hours was a person practising roller skating down the huge aisles. He commenced his routine by speed skating, pirouetting as a finale to complete his masterful performance. It was a good catch, but not what they were after. Perhaps the skater went on to greater things because GRP fabrication was not his forte. We never did learn his identity.

Then another man approached the telephone. He looked up and down the assembly shop and either side of the stanchion before he lifted the receiver. He dialled.

The security staff ran out from a vertical flap in the crate and over to the man, phone still in hand.

'What are you doing?' asked the security chief.

'Calling my auntie in Australia' was the man's answer. 'Everyone knows you can make outside calls from this phone.' And this was indeed what he was doing.

The hoaxer was never caught and the phone was changed to internal calls only. There were no more early finishes in the body shop.

Was the culprit Catholic or Protestant? We didn't know or care, but for some politicians in the community the even balance of employment between the religious groups was essential. Ian Paisley, the leader of the Protestant Democratic Unionist Party (DUP), maintained that the workers in the factory were predominantly

Catholic. A counter-claim from the Catholic communities suggested that they were in the minority. Only one thing would resolve it: a head count.

Ernie Benson spent three days working tirelessly with his colleagues, carefully sifting through personnel records, judging each employee's religion using his local knowledge and counting the score as he ticked off each name.

There are several ways to identify a person's religion in Belfast. If the address was Twinbrook, for instance, this would denote a Catholic, while a house in Seymour Hill would mean a Protestant employee. The unaccounted balance would then be sorted by the primary school noted on the employment application, primary schools being mainly sectarian. Any remnants after these two siftings would be judged on their first name or surname – Seamus or Oisean would be a Catholic, for sure, and there's nobody named Wesley or Boyd, to my knowledge, in the Catholic community.

The result was almost a dead heat, an outcome that surprised even the personnel department. They had lost track of the religious balance during their crash employment programme of summer 1981, trying to ramp up production to the target of 80 cars a day.

*Chapter 14*

# GOLD CARS AND OTHER DREAMS

During the short life of the company we were given some strange tasks to implement and others to review. We hoped that the DeLorean bus programme, designated DMC80, wouldn't come our way. Summer 1981 was really busy, as the start of production had been just six months earlier. Thankfully the bus programme never arrived at our stop. Neither did the Suzuki project, or the DMC44 off-highway vehicle.

Another of John DeLorean's ideas was a hi-fi system to be installed in the car with portable speakers to be used outside during picnics. Mike Loasby thought it would be terribly anti-social; fortunately John probably came round to this view as he didn't press the idea. Neither did he pursue the conversion of the rear luggage compartment into a refrigerator, although this programme did get past the idea stage. It was thought to be a real possibility, but was then dropped at the last moment. Plasma ignition didn't get far either. But the most audacious of all was the gold car programme.

It could only be John DeLorean who would commit to the manufacture of a car with gold panels and consider making a further hundred such vehicles without completing a feasibility study. In true DeLorean style he delegated working out the detail and practicality of the operation to those in the factory and beyond. The cars were to be made available to American Express in the US by late October 1981. According to Mike Knepper, director of public relations in New York, the idea for the gold car was probably the brainchild of Maur Dubin, John DeLorean's interior decorator.

Most of the management were hoping that it would be quietly forgotten, lost in the mists of time, as other ideas had been. But this scheme proved more durable.

The coating was to be 24-carat gold which is the purest form of the element, namely 99.9% gold. The first hurdle was to identify a plating facility prepared to undertake the task.

Stuart Craven, the most technically able of all the purchasing staff, was given the job of identifying a source and co-ordinating the project. Gold plating stainless steel panels was a formidable task and also unknown territory. Fortunately only three sets of panels were planned for the initial phase. Two were required for cars; the third would be a spare set if accidents occurred in transit or during assembly at Dunmurry.

Stuart located a supplier in Germany – Degussa. Payment for the work, including the cost of the gold, was to be up front and in full prior to Degussa starting any activity. This was necessary because the supplier didn't think the gold-plating process would work over such large areas and had thus demanded payment before disaster occurred – not afterwards, when there could be recriminations.

The cost of the large purpose-built vat was estimated at $37,000; the plating process added a further $15,000.

The cost of the gold itself was $45,000 so total charges, including ancillary costs, came to $131,000 ex-works for three sets of panels.

The amount of gold to be deposited on the panels increased to 860g (just under 2lb). At June 2012 prices the gold deposit on each car would have had a value of $44,000, but in 1981 it was a mere $15,000 per car.

Chuck Bennington, now new projects director, nominated Len Nelson from quality and George Frazer from material handling to support Stuart on the project. Stuart Craven takes up the story.

'In late July Degussa confirmed that they had test plated a metal sample and confirmed that they had achieved favourable results. However, they were sceptical about the project and suggested that we plate the sheet metal at the point of production to avoid damage to the surfaces after plating during transport or assembly of the parts. They would provide the know-how of the process, plus the electrolyte solution and specialists if required.

'On 20 August we held a meeting at Degussa with Herr Liebenow (commercial division) and Herr Schettle (technical). We covered the previous correspondence relating to the issues expected in plating such large parts, as their previous experience was with much thinner deposits of gold, 0.1 to 0.2 microns; the DeLorean requirement was 2.5 microns. They stated that they could not guarantee the gold could be evenly deposited over the panels and required a tolerance of +/– 2 microns.

'After lengthy discussions they agreed to commence plating in October. Degussa were to contact a sub-contractor to establish if the lead time could be improved and respond to us on Monday 24 August.

'Degussa replied that production was possible at a sub-contractor, but they would not accept any responsibility for the quality of the finished product. There were also other complications – the amount of electrolyte would have to increase along with the size of the plating tank, and drainage holes would be required in the doors and threaded inserts in the doors removed.

'The DeLorean operation at Dunmurry would provide personnel to certify that the panels were suitable for plating and satisfactory after plating. A comprehensive list of small parts was to be despatched to Degussa. Exhaust tail-pipe tips were to be designed and manufactured by Prescott Powell, a supplier based in England; road wheels were to be painted gold by Kent Alloys, and Phoenix GmbH in Hamburg agreed to paint the front and rear fascias to match a sample of sheet metal from the test piece.

'On completion of the plating process the panels were to be packed into tri-wall containers, shrink-wrapped in plastic and held in place with expanding foam. The vehicle-build programme was set to produce the cars, minus the exterior panels, by Tuesday 22 September, the date when the gold-plated parts were due to arrive in Dunmurry.

'Degussa insisted that their name was not to be used unless authorised by the company and that plating was to be completed and the electrolyte tank returned to Degussa by Saturday 19 September evening to avoid the additional cost of security guards.

'We arrived in Stuttgart on Tuesday 15 September and made our way to Holders factory in Unterlenningen. Upon arrival it became immediately clear as to why the plating was to be carried out there – the factory was on vacation for that week.

'As there was no labour available to assist us, we unpacked the panels so that they could be inspected prior to plating, but first we had to add paint lacquer on the inside of the panels to prevent the inner surfaces from being plated. Plating commenced on the Wednesday with the smallest panel, the roof T panel, followed by the front fenders.

'On Thursday we finished the re-plating of one of the roof panels and one front fender which had failed on gold thickness the previous day (the spec was for a minimum of 2.5 microns) and then started plating the rear fenders. We were making good progress, unpacking, cleaning, inspecting, lacquering, plating, inspecting and packing, but then just as things were going well, it happened…

'We opened the crate containing the doors, one of which had moved in transit, and we found a damaged corner. We immediately telephoned Dunmurry to arrange for a replacement door to be flown out, but this would not arrive until the end of the week and the plating had to be completed on Saturday.

'On Friday we started to plate the hoods, but we then hit another problem. Because the hood was so large, the time in the plating tank had to be increased to reach the minimum thickness of gold in the centre of the panel. This not only used up valuable time that we had planned for the doors, but the gold consumption also went up with a thickness of 4.21 microns being recorded at the edges.

'We also tried to repair the damaged door, but this was not successful; we just had to finish the five doors and leave the sixth until Saturday. We ran out of time on the Friday, only completing four of the doors.

'Early on Saturday I went with a driver to collect the door that had been flown over by special charter. It had arrived at 1800 hours on Friday evening, but there was no customs available to clear the goods. We were also told that customs clearance would not be available until Monday. I came out of the freight office into the hangar at Stuttgart airport and standing in the corner was the door. So with no one around I just picked the door up and walked out!

'We arrived back at Holder's when door number five had just completed the plating process, so with time running out we simply cleaned the door and put it straight into the plating tank without applying lacquer on the inside – so this door was plated on both sides. We completed the packing ready for loading into the truck.

'The plant manager commented that we could not ship the panels that night, as trucks were not allowed to travel on roads over the weekend in Germany. We showed him our transport, a refrigerated truck for fresh fruit; such vehicles were allowed on the road, but how the two drivers would get through customs at the border did not bear thinking about.

'Having driven non-stop from Germany the truck arrived early on Tuesday morning, and the final assembly of the two vehicles then began in a separate guarded facility in the DMCL factory.

'During the assembly process there were many problems. How could we remove water stains from the panels? What was the process for glazing on to gold plating? One door was damaged in the build process. There were also many small parts still to be gold plated – valves for the gold-painted wheels, reworked door hinges, rivets for the door seals, and so forth.

'The cars were completed on time and shipped to the USA. Customs clearance and onward transportation to the customer went smoothly. In an internal memo to Don Lander it was stated: "The San Francisco unit was in the hands of the dealer on Friday, and delivered to the customer on Monday 12 October. The customer was delighted and he and his wife drove the car from the dealer through San Francisco traffic to his home in Walnut Grove. The Texan customer has installed the unit in his bank and is very pleased with his car. His grand opening is on Thursday, 15 October."

'The final surprise came some weeks later. One of the small parts given to Degussa to plate was the DMC badge on the front of the car. This being an aluminium stamping, it was difficult to gold plate, but Degussa had finally succeeded in plating them and had sent two badges for the customers' cars and one for myself.'

The black cars to be used were built using the normal assembly process, then transferred to the gold crib in the EVP building at the rear of the Dunmurry site. Joe Murray blacked out the windows to stop prying eyes and photographers from witnessing the action. The operators and operatives who were allowed access to the area were provided with special gold car passes. Special overalls were ordered for those working on the car; these were without zips, buttons, hooks or buckles and used Velcro fasteners as a means of closing the overall together. No watches or rings were allowed to be worn in the crib, which had 24-hour security.

Some years later a sample was taken from one of the gold panels fitted to a car, to confirm the gold's purity. The result was certified by a recognised laboratory test house as 23.2-carat hard gold.

One of the two gold cars built at Dunmurry is currently in the Petersen Automotive Museum in Los Angeles, on loan from the Snyder National Bank. The second is located at the William F. Harrah Foundation/ National Automobile Museum in Reno, Nevada. The third set of panels was sold to Consolidated International, minus one door assembly, and used to convert a standard car to gold-plated panels to be sold in a raffle. As of 2012, this car is for sale with a sticker price of a quarter of a million dollars.

One final surprise awaits an owner of a gold car. On completion of the plating process Stuart Craven wrote an inscription from the New Testament on the inside of one of the doors. It reads: 'Your gold and silver is cankered; and the rust of them shall be a witness against you, and shall eat your flesh as it were fire. Ye have heaped treasure together for the last days' (James 5:3).

*Chapter 15*

# DOUBLING PRODUCTION AND THE EPISODE OF THE GOLD TAPS

M any of the senior staff were away on vacation in mid-August when Chuck invited me to attend a meeting he'd organised with Aldo Mantovani from Italdesign. Mantovani was one of the two founding members of Italdesign, Giorgetto Giugiaro being the more famous of the two legends. The topic for discussion was the four-seater DeLorean programme.

The sketches brought for review were of the DMC24, the four-seater, two-door DeLorean saloon. Not surprisingly, these pictured a car with two huge gull wing doors. The car looked tremendous, if not downright impracticable. The weight of the door on the current DMC was 80lb (36kg), but the ones in the sketches were almost double that size and weight. Chuck was his usual relaxed self in this auspicious company, and he spoke freely about the four-seat concept. John DeLorean was compiling a business plan which was to include changes to the DMC12 and the finances for introducing the DMC24. The total business plan was to be submitted to potential investors – including, of course, our main source of funds, the UK government.

Looking at the future in the presence of a legend of

the automotive industry was exciting, but day-to-day activities at the plant continued and occupied most of our time. In early August grey trim was introduced. The 1,700 plus cars shipped from the plant from the start of production until the end of July had all featured black trim. Other colours were planned but not scheduled to be introduced until early spring 1982, when the sales and marketing executives thought that alternative trim options would stimulate what they thought might by then be flagging sales.

The ramp-up to 80 cars a day, initiated in June, had looked impossible for the assembly staff to cope with, but the body shop had overcome their initial teething problems and were now producing black bodies to schedule. Several times during the month there was insufficient space in the body-holding area so the process had to be slowed down. This was a turnaround, because after Bobby Sands's death it had been the body shop whose production was hit hardest during the hunger strikes and funerals.

Although immense efforts were made by purchasing, materials management and the personnel department to ensure that resources were in place for manufacturing 80 cars a day, fewer than 50 cars per day were shipped in August. A major worry was that the influx of untrained labour in August and September might cause the quality of the finished product to deteriorate. For any manufacturing organisation the golden rule is not to allow the operators to use their initiative in the assembly process. This was a recipe for poor quality. But due to poor training, or no training at all, for both operators and supervisors initiative was the only way to get things moving. Work instructions were abandoned as the still rapidly changing specification of materials and constant modifications made these redundant. Once again we fell down the black hole of poor quality, although this time we knew why.

Meeting the new production programme was not a matter of survival, as it had been in January, but was now to satisfy John DeLorean's requirements for his public offering. His financial package would be unveiled to the world when we reached our peak of activity, which was estimated to be in a few months, possibly October.

One of the suppliers to cause problems which restricted output was the supplier of the plastic body mouldings on the exterior of the car, Phoenix GmbH in West Germany. The quality of the paint on the front and rear fascias was poor and the quality department rejected batch after batch. At one point we were rejecting up to 30% of all the material received. The parts were initially shipped back to Phoenix by road for reworking and repainting, but as the urgency for product increased more immediate methods of transport were required. By early September a dedicated daily flight was organised from Hamburg to Belfast. It would arrive late at night at Aldergrove and the parts would be ferried down to Dunmurry by truck. Fresh product would be unloaded and rejects reloaded on the same plane for return to Phoenix. The costs were immense, with Phoenix initially picking up the bill, although later in the year they attempted to obtain recompense.

By September most of the material procured for the higher volume scheduled two months earlier was being held either in the stores or outside on truck trailers. This excess material had a dual negative effect: space and cash flow. Raw material received from suppliers in September was due for payment at the end of October. In September output slowed once more as new and untrained labour was introduced in the altered shift patterns. Reduced output, of course, equates to reduced income.

The reduced output had a significant effect on the payment of bills. In September DMCL shipped 700 vehicles but received material for 1,600 cars. The financial avalanche had started, slowly at first, but then it picked up pace as the months ticked by. Financial trouble was heading towards us at a pace that we would be unable to control.

To complicate matters we introduced the single key system in September. Initially this was a disaster. Earlier cars had a double key system, one for the ignition and another for the doors. With the two-key system the production line could take any matching pair of doors at random. Now things were different, because with a single key system the body assembly complete with ignition lock and doors had to match. Often the matching door lock wasn't ready due to quality failure or non-availability of material. To overcome the problem a previous quality-approved pair of doors would have the locks changed to allow a passing vehicle to be fitted with doors. It's for this reason that a DeLorean owner may see a VIN (Vehicle Identification Number) on the roof panel of the door crossed out and another number written in its place. This was a common occurrence after September 1981.

The single key system caused chaos, and again it was Harry Steadman who was called in to sort out the problem. Tirelessly enthusiastic, Harry would always be the last man in the assembly area, sorting out this and other manufacturing problems. He seemed to have forgotten where he lived, as many did who worked on site.

We were now employing an additional 200 people per week. The data systems couldn't keep pace with the rate of change. Not only were bills of materials and process sheets hopelessly out of date by the time they were printed but also wages were not being paid as the significant number of new recruits was too much for the payroll system. Ernie Benson from the DeLorean personnel department recalls that because we couldn't arrange pay packets for new starters on time each Friday, the workers who had not been paid queued to give details of their working week. They were asked how many hours they had worked. A quick calculation was made and the employee would be given a cheque for the appropriate amount; then a record of the payment was logged on the employee's details, and so on, until the system coped with the wage issue.

Paying the wages was not the only problem to cross Don Lander's desk that month. A more alarming and potentially destructive problem made the headlines on Monday 4 October 1981. DeLorean Motor Cars Ltd and their officers were to be investigated for alleged misuse of public funds.

The enquiry was initiated because of revelations supplied to a prominent Conservative MP, Nicholas

Winterton. These allegations originated from Marion Gibson, a secretary and deputy administrator in the New York office. In her last job at DMC she had worked for Bill Haddad. One of the key exhibits of the exposé was a private memo written by Bill to John DeLorean during the Christmas break of 1980.

Marion Gibson made allegations of impropriety, but the words that made headlines were gold faucets (taps) purchased for the Warren House, the residence of the managing director of DMCL. (They were subsequently identified as being gold plated and purchased from a supplier in central London.)

Someone in the factory started a rumour that police from Scotland Yard's fraud squad had arrived and were interviewing key witnesses in the offices. It wasn't true, but the story spread around the plant quickly. Officers from the Metropolitan Police had turned up in New York; none came to Belfast.

By the end of the following week it became clear that there would be no arrests or prosecutions and no police investigation. We heard on the BBC news that John was suing anyone who'd had a hand in the story. He had hired Lord Goodman, one of the UK's leading lawyers, known as 'the power behind the throne', to pursue and prosecute the guilty, but the news had hit the headlines even harder than the first story of allegations of misappropriation of government money. The bad press continued, day after day, week after week, even though it could have been buried immediately after the police review had been halted by Mrs Thatcher.

Once again, the bull had run through the china shop.

Life continued within the factory, however, and we were making progress, with 1,800 cars shipped in October, our biggest volume month since the start of production. It's possible that our performance and renewed credibility at that time swayed the government into avoiding an unnecessary and prolonged public enquiry or police investigation

For the first and probably the last time we were being viewed as a successful company.

Bache Halsey Stuart Shield, the brokerage firm underwriting the public stock issue, agreed to a delay, to wait for a better climate for DeLorean affairs, allowing the current buzz in the press to quieten down. The Marion Gibson affair was too fresh in the minds of the public. A few months' delay would be a much better time for the launch – say after Christmas, in early 1982?

It seems likely that without the affair of the gold taps the public stock offering would have progressed according to plan and the flotation would have been a huge success ... at least for a few months. We were riding high as a company in October 1981. Production was at its peak and there were no major concerns, or at least none that were publicised.

Unknown to many, however, the finances of the company were in poor health and another major injection of cash was required.

*Chapter 16*

# GOLDEN OCTOBER TO WHITE DECEMBER: CRACKS APPEAR

The saga of the gold taps was behind us and we now seemed to have a bright future. Our critics would be silenced once we became profitable, which we believed was just around the corner. What else could the world throw at us? We had been through every imaginable scenario of disaster. We felt nothing could stop us now – we were on our way to success.

By October 1981 we had shipped 4,343 cars with a value of £76 million; of these, 1,800 were shipped in October. We now employed 2,557 operatives and a further 76 canteen and security personnel, with 3,000 more people involved in the material supply chain. The local community – butchers, bakers, grocery stores, local small businesses, pubs, restaurants – were all feeding off the DeLorean factory and had never known business to be so good.

The DeLorean wage bill was £17 million per annum. We'd taken half of our employees from the social security register, therefore lessening the government's financial burden of funding the unemployed and their households. The double bonus for the government was that now the former unemployed, rather than receiving social security payments from government coffers, were net contributors to the exchequer, for some £6.3 million was planned to be sent to the government in personal tax revenues in 1981. Under the terms of the master agreement further income came to the government, with royalties from the sale of cars amounting to £205,350 in June and another payment due soon.

John DeLorean had promised that employment in the factory would increase to between 3,500 and 4,000 in 1982 and we believed him. The four-seat DMC24 was to be launched in 1983/84 and initial discussions with Italdesign, in which I was playing a part, looked promising.

Plans to extend the factory were made and a business plan was submitted to the government for the next three years showing significant income and profit. A change to ERM for the main structure was reviewed.

The design detail of the body, chassis and interior trim components was stabilising and we were regularly producing 80 cars a day. That was fortunate because Dick Brown, the sales director in the US, was demanding more cars. The £84 million invested by the UK government was paying off.

The gold cars were completed and shipped to the US on a Boeing 747 in early October.

On 21 October John DeLorean attended the Earls Court car show in London, our first entry in this prestigious exhibition, the highlight of the UK automotive year. Things looked good and the future seemed exciting.

By late October George Lacey, the engineering director, and Dick Brown were exchanging correspondence to agree a list of changes to be incorporated in the 1982 model. We were now looking forward to planned product changes rather than fighting daily battles to survive, with never-ending engineering changes. Did we ever build two cars to the same specification?

Meanwhile, the management profile was looking different from that of two years earlier. Gene Cafiero left the company on 15 December with a generous leaving package, his departure a quiet affair with no farewell speeches. Chuck Bennington had also resigned in November. Bill Haddad had his last argument with John DeLorean. Bill's memo of Christmas 1980 highlighted extravagant expenditure in Belfast, and he voiced his concerns to DeLorean regarding the GPD contract, causing irreconcilable differences between the two. Bill had also resisted the formation of the new holding company planned by John and courageously told him where he was going wrong. To my knowledge, he was the only senior executive to make a stand. Bob Donnell had left, taking Martin Graham with him to Bombardier in Shannon in the south of Ireland.

However, unknown to many in the company, our finances were going downhill at an alarming rate. Cash flow is always a good indication of financial stability and ours showed we weren't paying our suppliers to a reasonable timescale – and payments were slipping further as the weeks ticked by. The outlook was poor. Events were now unfolding that would lead to receivership in four months' time.

Back in Belfast a NIDA board meeting in late October started a process of facing up to John DeLorean, calling his bluff and stopping further waste of public funds. At least that's how the civil servants would see the picture.

The NIDA board meeting took place at 100 Belfast Road, Maryfield, Holywood, Belfast. This location was accessed by a left turn from the Sydenham bypass in Holywood into what might appear to a passing motorist to be a leafy suburban avenue, a small residential complex with smart houses in a fashionable cul-de-sac, except for the fact that it was positioned next to Palace Barracks, home to the British army in Northern Ireland for the previous 60 years and from 2009 officially the headquarters of MI5 in Northern Ireland. The NIDA offices were in a secure location for the senior civil servants to gather for their monthly meetings.

NIDA executives were desperate to obtain reliable financial information from DeLorean, but nothing appeared for some time. The master agreement with the government specified that quarterly accounts should be submitted to NIDA within two months from the end of any accounting period. DeLorean was in default. If and when financial reports were made they were usually optimistic and implausible. The continuous DeLorean rhetoric of grand plans and massive profitability without tangible, realistic accounts was now driving the NIDA officials to despair. John DeLorean thought he had a credible answer for every difficult question. Civil servants often doubted their own wisdom as John's arguments were often initially plausible – but very few could hold water.

The next NIDA meeting, on 25 November, debated many subjects to be discussed with John DeLorean on his next visit to Northern Ireland. All of them were negative.

Why was Gene Cafiero given such a significant

leaving settlement? Also, what was John DeLorean doing to reduce the cost of the operations in the US, now running at a total of $800,000 per month? Dick Brown's quality control centres in the USA were soaking up money at an alarming rate and the excessive labour costs at the plant in Dunmurry were also worrying. The funding of the DeLorean New York office, at over $200,000 per month, caused considerable strain on the cash flow and profitability of the operation too.

Further embarrassment occurred when the DMC board approved total bonuses of $760,000 for the board of directors, with $101,000 for John DeLorean himself, $76,000 to Thomas Kimmerley (lawyer and senior vice-president of DMC in New York) and lesser amounts down the hierarchy's pecking order. To NIDA's embarrassment, the two local Belfast businessmen appointed to the board had seconded the motion to pay out the money. The NIDA officials were furious. All confidence and credibility had now disappeared. John DeLorean now had no supporters this side of the Atlantic, or at least none that could save him from the decline into the abyss of receivership that was becoming inevitable. Personal greed would bring disaster to us all.

The DeLorean empire was starved of cash and the government's bank guarantees would expire at the end of the year. The company needed money, and quickly. NIDA would give John no more cash, but after negotiation they did agree to extend the bank guarantees to a lesser amount. However, that was to be it – there would be no more money. DeLorean's request for export financing (ECGD) was once again refused, as was his request for a further £40 million in grant aid to allow operations in Belfast to continue.

John DeLorean was planning a visit to Northern Ireland in mid-December. NIDA meant to make this a visit for him to remember, a reminder that the pot, at least John DeLorean's pot, was empty and there was definitely no more money.

The NIDA board meeting discussed other Northern Ireland industrial matters. The situation at Short Brothers, the aircraft and missile manufacturer based just a few miles from the DeLorean factory, was a major topic. The details were confirmed in Parliament by Jim Prior, in December 1981, when he reported that borrowings for Short Brothers up to March 1981 had been £30 million. Later NIDA approved further funding to Harland and Wolff, just down the road from Short Brothers.

Back at the Dunmurry plant, however, things still looked good, at least to many of us working at the coal face. We produced 800 cars in December but shipped less; what we didn't see was the build-up of inventory at the docks in both Belfast and the USA. The storm was brewing but we didn't yet know that this was to be the peak of the good times at DMCL.

In early December a scene that was not to occur too often took place in the manufacturing area. A group of senior staff, mainly directors, assembled adjacent to the chassis assembly line outside the metallurgical laboratory. I was invited to join the small gathering. The directors were grouped around a rolling chassis. The topic of discussion was DeLorean's recall notice – headed 'Motor Vehicle Defect Report' – submitted to the US National Traffic Highway Safety Administration (NHTSA) on 9 November. This concerned a problem with the front suspension. The product recall detailed the replacement of the ball-joint retaining nut and involved drilling the ball-joint shaft to allow a pin to be inserted to stop the retaining nut unwinding and in the process collapsing the suspension. There were over 2,000 cars built that required rework.

Unfortunately the nut provided with the recall cracked when drilled. The cause of the problem was that these nuts had not been heat-treated during manufacture to relieve tensions after plating. It was a basic procedure, but someone had forgotten to add the process to the manufacturing plan, an expensive and embarrassing mistake on a two-cent item that initiated a recall on an existing recall. This was a first in automotive history.

Don Lander was present at the gathering, and he was incandescent with rage, pointing with his finger at anyone who would meet his gaze. Diplomatically I stood to the rear of the crowd, allowing the directors the first chance of a reply. The employees on the line were watching the scene unfold, and they seemed to be enjoying the drama of Don reprimanding the senior staff in full view of the hourly paid workers and demonstrating that management could also be subject to admonishment. There were many senior heads staring at the floor that morning while Don was in full flight. The Christmas spirit had yet to arrive in Dunmurry.

Despite this setback, during the last few days of December we went about our business with some confidence that we had made progress. The saddle-brown trim was planned for introduction at the end of February, burgundy in mid-April and blue at the end of April 1982. CP Trim had submitted samples for approval and the colours made a wonderful change from black and grey.

Then came a surprise visit on 15 December (all visits of dignitaries to Northern Ireland were, of course, subject to security arrangements), when the Secretary of State, James Prior, came to the plant. This first meeting between James Prior and John DeLorean didn't get off to a good start. John had decided to stay in London the previous night and travel to Belfast in the morning, but bad weather delayed his plane and he arrived at the factory two hours late. This didn't endear him to Mr Prior. Just how many cups of coffee can a Secretary of State drink to pass the time? Later than scheduled they toured the plant, and James Prior was clearly impressed. On leaving he thanked John for the employment he was giving to the people in the area. It was looking like another scalp on John DeLorean's belt. But the feeling of relief and optimism was premature, as we were to witness after the Christmas break.

On Friday evening, 18 December, the staff Christmas party took place at the Conway hotel, just across the street from the DMCL factory. John DeLorean gave a speech and emphasised the need for improved quality and for us to maintain our high production rate because the sales people in the US could sell every car that we could make. The festivities continued for some hours, with a final speech given by a new US board member which finished with the statement: 'We are all going to be very rich.' (We knew that this was the royal 'we', as used by Queen Victoria when referring to herself alone.) Given the amount of liquid sustenance we had enjoyed over the previous few hours, we clapped and cheered with relish.

We weren't expecting to make our fortunes at DeLorean, however; we would just be happy to keep our jobs. The return from the Christmas break in early January 1982 would shatter that illusion.

The snow was falling in Belfast on 23 December 1981 when I flew out of Aldergrove airport to return home for the Christmas holidays. I was looking forward to an exciting New Year.

I wasn't to be disappointed.

*Chapter 17*

# DARK WINTER DAYS AND RECEIVERSHIP

In the first week of January Arctic winds swept southwards across the United Kingdom, with heavy snow falling over a wide area of central Scotland, Northern Ireland and England. It was not a good omen for the start of the year – and the weather was much worse in the northern states of America. It was the hardest and longest spell of cold weather in the US for a hundred years. Cars don't sell when snow is on the ground. Add the recession still biting western economies to that equation, plus the fact that the DeLorean car was now being advertised at a much higher selling price than originally envisaged, and the result for DeLorean Motor Cars Ltd was disaster.

The weather also made life difficult for other car makers, of course. In January 1982 all but one of Ford's 17 assembly plants were closed, all five of Chrysler's plants were shut due to poor sales, and eight out of GM's 32 factories closed or were working a short week. Sales of cars in the UK were the worst for four years.

The $30 million credit facility agreed with the Bank of America to fund shipments had expired. Moreover, John DeLorean and his company were now in default because the last shipment of cars was made without payment, a process forbidden in the master agreement.

The loan guarantee underwritten by the British government after the Portakabin fire in May the previous year had also expired. Unable to finance further shipments, and in reality not requiring any further vehicles to be made, John DeLorean considered the future.

On 6 January 1982 Bache Halsey Stuart Shield, the underwriting brokerage firm, asked for a second postponement of the public stock offering because the rumours in the marketplace were that the car was not selling.

There was gossip in the factory that cars were being stockpiled in the docks at Belfast and also in North America. How was this possible? Only three weeks earlier, at the staff Christmas party, John DeLorean had told us that the future looked bright and the sales department was calling for more cars. What had gone wrong?

We now received a daily diet of news from the media, particularly the *Belfast Telegraph*, but the really big story came from the *Guardian* newspaper on 6 January when they reported that John DeLorean was looking for a partner to either invest in or take over the company. He approached Lee Iacocca for perhaps the second time during the short life of the DeLorean venture. Iacocca records the meeting in his book *Iacocca: An Autobiography*. He turned down John's idea to amalgamate the two companies with the words 'two losers together is not a good idea'. John also approached General Motors for assistance. After the publication of *On a Clear Day You Can See General Motors* three years earlier he probably received a reception equal to that of the temperature outside.

Once again John DeLorean complained that the absence of ECGD (Export Credit Guarantee Department) funding had caused the financial problem, arguing that the cost of financing shipment of cars through the Bank of America was much higher than it would have been with ECGD support. We all knew that financing shipments was not the root cause of the problem, however. Only sales to customers would eventually improve cash flow. John DeLorean's take on the ECGD issue was a means of sidestepping the main problem and passing the responsibility to the UK government.

As the finance department in Belfast had stopped taking calls the suppliers were again phoning their contacts in purchasing to seek assistance on payment and to be fed the latest news. There was little we could do. We didn't control the purse strings or the communication channels. Payments were now being made for essential supplies only. At one point in mid-January General Motors, a significant supplier of parts, had suspended shipments until their bills were paid. After pointing out to GM that suspension of supplies could result in the demise of DMCL, and that they might be deemed to be responsible, they relented and agreed to supply one more consignment. However, if bills were not paid after this shipment no further material would be shipped. This was the last shipment of parts from GM.

We realised that support from the community was essential in lobbying the government, so in an effort to keep the local traders on our side we paid as many of these smaller accounts as cash flow would allow.

With the shortage of cash and the high stock of unsold vehicles we were told to cut back production, implementing the plan without delay. By chance a strike at Sealink, who operated one of the ferry crossings between England and Ireland, began on 8 January and halted the movement of containers from mainland Britain to Ireland. This dispute was used as an excuse to cut back on production: essential supplies for the plant were held in England and could not be shipped across the Irish Sea. This was the story we were to tell, if asked.

We knew this to be untrue as another ferry company not involved in the dispute, Townsend Thoresen, would have been able to carry the supplies. The reality was, of course, that we didn't need the parts because we had a significant stock of material to take us through the much reduced production programme.

On 11 January the 'lack of supplies due to the seamen's strike' story led to the workforce being placed on a three-day week. We gave that official communication out to suppliers but knew that the story would eventually be identified as a lie. As predicted, it made matters worse as up to that point our personal credibility with the supply base was high.

John DeLorean had clearly not read the script because he announced to the world's press that the whole matter was caused by the lack of ECGD funding and that it was the UK government's fault. That scuppered the seamen's strike argument. It was a pity that both sides of the Atlantic were not telling the same story – putting out a joint release would have helped us all. We were now as confused as the suppliers. DMCL was beginning to lose credibility, and fast.

The next day the quality centres in the US cut back on the staff employed to check and rework cars, explaining that the quality of the product now being received from Dunmurry had dramatically improved and that there was no longer any need for the rigorous quality checks and reworks. The truth was much simpler; there was little or no money available to fund the US quality centres.

By 13 January the seamen's strike had been settled, so seemingly there was now no reason not to return to full production. The workforce, the government and the unions were not fooled, however, and sensed a major problem; they were just not privy to the details. The suppliers weren't fooled either, because most of them had not been paid for months.

One local Northern Ireland supplier made their own arrangements to cover their debt. Northern Ireland Carriers (NIC) were contracted to move cars from the factory to Belfast docks. In early 1982, realising that the DeLorean factory was heading for receivership, NIC took unilateral action to recover their debt by hijacking cars in transit. Neal Barclay, who loaded the cars on to the transporters, gives further details of the story.

'Three car carriers left the company at Dunmurry late morning, each loaded with six cars on each transporter. It was the intent of the NIC management to divert all three trucks as they passed a certain point in their journey to the NIC yard and impound the cars as a lien against the debt. At a critical junction in the road network an NIC manager stepped in front of the car carrier to stop and divert the first truck, but the driver missed the signal to turn, going on to his original destination at the docks. The next two drivers caught the manager's signals and eventually diverted the trucks into the NIC yard. Twelve cars were seized.'

Denis Boyle, Neal's boss, phoned Billy McCallam at the DeLorean office at the docks. The transporters had left the DeLorean site over two hours ago and had not yet arrived. What had happened? Then the story unfolded.

Protests from the company that the vehicles had been taken unlawfully were dismissed by NIC; a subsequent legal case brought by the company (during receivership) failed to obtain legal title for DMCL. NIC won the battle and the vehicles were put up for sale at the Culloden hotel on 14 September 1982. According to Robert Lamrock, who was present at the auction, the cars were sold for between £10,500 and £15,300.

On 18 January 1982 John DeLorean had a meeting with government officials in London. They were less than sympathetic about DeLorean affairs because other problems in Northern Ireland had caught their attention. Short Brothers, the aircraft manufacturer based only a few miles from the DeLorean plant, was about to announce job losses of 650 staff; this followed the 300 who'd been made redundant three months earlier. Short Brothers still employed 6,000 workers and were regarded as Northern Ireland's premier blue-chip organisation. It was impossible for the government to support jobs at DeLorean and ignore the job losses at Short Brothers. It was a major dilemma.

That week we counted only 140 DeLorean cars completed and ready for shipment, but they were going nowhere – except the backyard of the factory or the docks.

We were eager for news about the future of the company and read everything possible on the subject in order to find something to cling on to, a ray of hope. The *Belfast Telegraph* reported that John DeLorean was to meet government officials on 20 January at the Dunmurry plant to discuss the way forward. The newspaper stated that their sources in the government suggested it would be more inclined to invest in the company if the sales, manufacturing and design rights of the car were in the hands of UK investors. The master agreement, signed in 1978, had confirmed that the sales rights in the US belonged to John DeLorean and the design rights of the DMC12 to the Oppenheimer group of original investors.

We waited for this news to break, but again it was a non-event. Later that day the government approved a further guarantee on loans but only for £10 million, and by mid-year 1982 this figure would reduce to £5 million. John DeLorean was demanding £40 million in non-returnable grants. The gap in financing requirements and credibility was so large that it was unlikely any kind of settlement could be salvaged from the talks.

The problem drifted on over the next few weeks. The reality was that sales of the car, from the start of production to the third week of January 1982, comprised a total of 4,756 vehicles, of which 3,085 were with customers. The total number shipped from Belfast was 7,400, with a further 435 in transit. There was unsold stock of 4,750 cars, or three months' output from the factory.

DeLorean matters deteriorated further when an article published in mid-January by *Private Eye* magazine, the UK's leading satirical publication, and read by government and opposition, banks and politicians, gave details of one of John DeLorean's key staff members and one of his closest friends, Roy Nesseth. His criminal history was recorded in detail. Photocopies of the article were circulated through the office. I had met Roy Nesseth several months earlier during one of his visits to Dunmurry; he was big, rather strange and the sort of man with whom you didn't argue. How could the details in the magazine be true? This was someone who was a close friend and confidant of John DeLorean, who in turn many believed to be as close to a saint as it was possible to be on God's earth. The writer must have got it wrong. Regrettably, however, the details were true, as we were to learn later.

On 21 January James Prior met John DeLorean and told him that he intended to commission a report from Coopers and Lybrand and Cork Gully regarding the future prospects of the company. These were two leading city consultancies, and the work was to be undertaken by Paul Shewell of Coopers and Lybrand and Sir Kenneth Cork of Cork Gully. The review was to cover all aspects of the company, including manufacturing, sales and finance activities.

Kenneth Bloomfield, representing the Department of Commerce in Northern Ireland, confirmed this when he wrote to John DeLorean on 22 January 1982 outlining the concerns of both the Department of Commerce and the government. 'On the basis of the facts at present available to the government, there must be serious doubts about the continuing viability of the companies... This is a matter of serious concern for the government.' The suggestion was that Sir Kenneth Cork would review the viability of the operation and report back within two weeks.

In the House of Commons on 28 January 1982 Bob Cryer made a comment regarding the transfer of government money intended for the DeLorean factory to an overseas account. The amount mentioned was £9 million, transferred to a bank in Panama. This sowed the seeds of doubt regarding the integrity of John DeLorean and would be the start of the trail to find the missing GPD equity money.

On 29 January Don Lander, DeLorean's managing director at Dunmurry, announced that 1,100 jobs were to go. There was an immediate outcry from the community. The priests from St Luke's Church in Twinbrook said that this would be a disaster for the area, with the long-term employed only just starting to reap the rewards of employment from the DeLorean plant. Young families had taken out mortgages on new homes based upon their newly found wealth and would now be unable to meet the payments. Priests and other community leaders urged the government to continue supporting the DeLorean project. For many it would be their second redundancy in as many years. First from Grundig, then DeLorean.

There was further bad news for Northern Ireland. Mackies Ltd, another major employer in Belfast, announced redundancies of 600 staff; these were to be effective immediately.

On 3 February sympathetic Members of Parliament –
there were some, but not many – asked the government
to do everything possible to save the plant, reminding
them that a further 3,000 jobs with suppliers in
mainland Britain were also at risk.

In Birmingham on Saturday 6 February a meeting
of the UK DeLorean suppliers creditors' group, held to
co-ordinate action, urged the government to recognise
the sales potential of the DeLorean car. The event was
organised by John Putt, managing director of Barrett
Engineers, a major supplier to the DeLorean factory in
Dunmurry. It's interesting to note that in their press
release there was an absence of a request to call for
support for John DeLorean's company; it just recognised
that the DMC12 had sales potential. This was a clear
message from the UK suppliers that they would only
support the Dunmurry company if John DeLorean was
not involved in any future reconstruction plan. A similar
message was sent by the Northern Ireland DeLorean
creditors' group, led by Malcolm Stevens.

John Putt played a major role in organising the supply
base and keeping them informed of events. He met
James Prior on a number of occasions to show supplier
support for the continuation of production at the factory.
Months later, John Putt's role in representing the
suppliers was key to the receiver retaining confidence
in the future prospects of the company in Dunmurry;
without him, the receiver might have given up any
chance of salvaging the company months earlier.

At one point during the discussions with the
government John DeLorean offered to give the UK
government all his financial stock, saying he would

walk away with nothing. What he didn't say was that he held the distribution rights to the car in the United States and these would remain with him, while the rights to the car itself were owned by the Oppenheimer partnership and therefore not within his gift to transfer. These hollow words were meant to attract public support and sympathy and change the direction of flak that was being aimed towards him, redirecting it to Sir Kenneth Cork and the UK government.

On 12 February 1,100 workers left the factory for the last time, as planned two weeks earlier. Among them were Bridie Johnston, who worked on the engine dress line, and Geraldine Maxwell. Both still maintain today that John DeLorean was the innocent party. Joe Murray and his wife Eileen both lost their jobs later, during receivership, and again both regard John DeLorean as blameless.

Many of the dismissed workers belonged to the same household, for it was not unusual for three people from the same family to be working at the DeLorean factory. This was a nightmare bigger than John DeLorean could ever imagine. Unemployment benefit was £41.50 per person per week. For many this was less than a third of their pay at DeLorean. It was a major disaster for the local community, too. Local shops witnessed an immediate downturn in trade, as did the small manufacturing and support companies feeding the DeLorean staff; some closed their doors for good.

But, for the time being, 1,500 people remained employed at the factory.

Suppliers anxious about receiving payment continued to phone their contacts in purchasing to seek assistance in getting hold of their money. We continued to take calls from suppliers, most of whom we knew from our previous lives in the car industry. We could only relay the information that we had to hand. The things we couldn't offer were payment, optimism and comfort.

By mid-February Sir Kenneth Cork released his report to the government; this included a comment that the maximum annual sales potential of the DMC12 was probably in the region of 8,000 cars for the US (this was less than half of our maximum production rate) with 1,500 in Canada and a further 2,000 in Europe. The figures were similar to J.D. Power's estimates in its original report to John DeLorean at the launch of the company three years earlier; the purpose of that report had been to identify volumes that could be expected from varying selling prices of the car.

More alarmingly, during his review of the company's short history Sir Kenneth Cork uncovered details of misappropriation of funds that he believed had originated in the early days of the DeLorean–Chapman deal. Further investigation on this issue would wait for a few months, when the case of the missing money was to be looked at in more detail. On 16 February Sir Kenneth Cork commented: 'DeLorean (Cars Limited) has a future – but urgently needs an injection of money.'

James Prior planned to make a statement in the House of Commons on 19 February regarding the future of the company. We knew that his comments would determine our future. Someone brought a portable radio into the Coventry office and we all crowded round, waiting for him to speak. A few minutes after 11am Jim Prior announced that the company would enter receivership (a legal entity similar to Chapter 11 in the US). This was a huge relief as we'd feared the worst; immediate closure would not have been a surprise. We chatted for some time about the ramifications of receivership. The compensation for us was that we would receive no further phone calls from suppliers requesting payment; there was no point in them calling because all authority was now handed over to the receiver as absolute controller of both the company and our destiny.

John DeLorean's press release to the dealers in the US following the announcement could, to the untrained eye, be seen as positive. In summary it said: 'DeLorean Motor Cars Ltd and the Northern Ireland government today reached agreement to the continued production of the DeLorean automobile at the government's plant in Dunmurry – James Prior has expressed his full support in this extremely advantageous reorganisation. This new foundation ensures continuity of production. The government has removed $130,000,000 of government debt from the company's balance sheet. The company made a profit of $6 million in the quarter ended 31 August and operating profit of $4 million in the last quarter.' There was no mention of receivership in the communication and it looked from this press release as though the reorganisation was John DeLorean's own idea.

The receiver, Sir Kenneth Cork, arrived at Dunmurry on 19 February; Shaun Harte greeted him at the entrance to the factory. Shaun was the only board member remaining on site. The other senior directors had either left the company or were at DeLorean headquarters in the US; most were never seen again.

▲ *The DeLorean factory in early summer 1981. The body shop can be seen top left, the assembly building top right, the fabrication building bottom left, and the Emissions and Vehicle Preparation building (EVP) bottom right. The Twinbrook housing estate is alongside the factory at the top of the picture.* (Tony Swann)

▼ *The test track. Notice the banked rear shoulder with Armco barrier.* (Tony Swann)

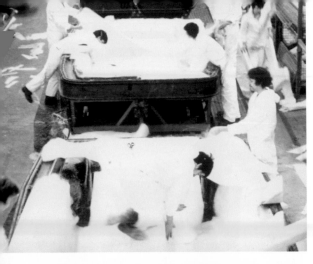

◀ *Laying up continuous-filament glass-fibre matt into the VARI mould at the body shop.*
(Tony Swann)

◀ *Mating the male and female parts of the mould prior to resin injection.*
(Matt Sommer)

◀ *Lotus Cars mould shop: VARI manufacture of an Esprit body with low capital investment.*
(Lotus Cars)

▲ *The clinch press for the assembly of the inner and outer door.* (Matt Sommer)

▼ *Assembling the inner door components.* (Matt Sommer)

▲ *Fitting the gull wing doors in the assembly shop.* (Matt Sommer)

▼ *Adding the stainless panels and the front and rear fascia panels on the Tellus carrier.* (Tony Swann)

▶ *The final assembly stage: adding the wheels. Notice the Tellus control tower on the top left of the photograph.*
(Tony Swann)

▶ *The Emissions and Vehicle Preparation building (EVP), which was initially used as a repair hospital for cars requiring rework.*
(Tony Swann)

▶ *The high-pressure water test.*
(Tony Swann)

▲*This photograph of early cars was taken around February 1981. Passenger doors were taped to prevent water ingress. Some cars were scavenged for good parts and then rebuilt at the QC centres in the US.* (Tony Swann)

▼ *The flag that annoyed John DeLorean. The DeLorean car bursting through the letter H represented the Maze prison block where those on hunger strike were imprisoned.* (Pacemaker Press)

▲ *One of only two gold cars on the test track – film crews and the press were in attendance.* (Tony Swann)

▼ *Stuart Craven and Len Nelson from DMCL unpacking stainless steel panels prior to gold-plating at Holden GmbH in Germany.* (Stuart Craven)

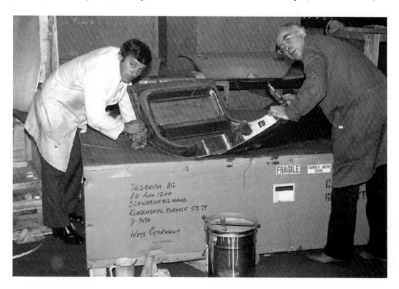

▲ *Captain O'Donnell, master of the* Severn Princess, *took this photograph. It records the ditching of the DeLorean dies once used to press the stainless steel panels.* (Captain O'Donnell)

▲ *The author (left) and Harry Steadman in 2011. Harry was one of the key players involved in building the factory and the car.* (Harry Steadman)

▼ *The author (right) with Dixon Hollinshead, the driving force behind the building of the factory – ahead of schedule. This photo was taken at the Dunmurry site at Eurofest DeLorean car show in 2011.* (Nick Sutton)

▼ *The fabulous D-Rex, designed and engineered by Rich Weissensel.* (Rich Weissensel)

Sir Kenneth spoke to the management team and the shop stewards before touring the factory. He was clearly impressed, as everyone always was who visited the site. The cleanliness of the plant and the industrious nature of the workforce were our biggest selling factors. This was not a British Leyland plant with antiquated machinery and a workforce indifferent to their employer's success. This was DeLorean Motor Cars Ltd in Belfast, a modern factory with all those employed anxious to get on with making cars. No one could fail to be impressed. The hourly paid workers were our prime asset, something that Sir Kenneth immediately recognised. It was probably not what he was expecting to see.

The fact that a notable English figure, well known and respected in government and financial circles, arrived in Belfast and talked to the hourly paid operatives endeared him to everyone he met. He became a passionate supporter of the DeLorean community in Dunmurry, although less enthusiastic about John DeLorean; the feeling was apparently mutual.

Sir Kenneth wanted this to be a constructive receivership. He hoped it would save the business because of the distress it would cause in Northern Ireland, with the associated loss of jobs of which many would never be replaced. We believed in the sincerity of this man. His first instruction was to arrange that the 500 part-completed cars in production be converted to finished products, a process he envisaged would take three months.

We lasted significantly longer than that, thanks to Sir Kenneth Cork.

## Chapter 18

# RECOVERY PLANS AND EMPLOYEE NUMBER 21

Very little happened for some time after receivership. Purchasing staff were told to put on hold any tooling investment in the process of being completed and to stop all activities with suppliers that would incur further debt. The receiver required a summary of all tooling and capital commitments from the start of the programme to the day of receivership. The completed list showed a total investment with suppliers for production parts tooling of £12.4 million, most of which had been paid.

The silence at the DeLorean Coventry office was strange and unnerving. There had been three years of frantic activity, engineering changes, answering requests for status on new or modified parts, phone calls from suppliers demanding payment, travelling to Belfast, Lotus or suppliers. Now there was nothing. There was a lack of noise and, more importantly, a lack of urgency in the air. The atmosphere felt similar to bereavement. Over the next few weeks the mood became tense – we didn't know what to expect, when the axe would fall and on whom. We read the newspapers for signs of a saviour or a change of heart by the government. Initially there were daily press reports of actions in the US and theories in the leader columns as to the next step. As time passed the news on all things DeLorean faded as the press lost interest. We were no longer on the front pages. Perhaps this was the government's plan, slowly and deliberately to allow the company to fade away with as little fuss as possible. This was our biggest fear.

In early March we heard of Ken Gorf's problems in the United States. Ken had been treasurer of the Belfast facility, reporting to Joe Daly, but he had elected to work in the US some months earlier, to assist in the financial control of the company there. This was an area where NIDA had major concerns, and Ken was there to bring some discipline and order.

On 8 March he sent a message from California saying that he was concerned regarding the lack of financial control at the US operations. He listed numerous areas of concern to Joe Daly, the finance director, among them that door locks had been changed on the Irvine facility in California and that he was no longer a key holder. Ken left the company shortly afterwards.

Full details of the story emerged later. Dick Brown had been fired and Bruce McWilliams was now in charge of sales and marketing. Dick Brown's leaving package consisted solely of a threat to him and his family, relayed to him by Roy Nesseth on the phone from the Waldorf Hotel in New York. The locks were changed at the QAC centre in Irvine, California to stop Dick and his sympathisers from entering the buildings.

On the east coast cars from the DeLorean Bridgewater facility were taken by armed force and ferried by car transporter to John DeLorean's Bedminster estate. A similar attempt to remove cars was made in Irvine. The Bank of America, who financed and owned the cars in transit, until sold, submitted a court order issued by Judge Brieant on 9 March for the return of the vehicles.

Budget-Rent-A-Car entered the scene as a potential buyer of unsold DeLoreans. As internal communication within the company had all but broken down we read reports of the progress with Budget from the national newspapers. Discussions with them continued for a month or so until they became aware that financial title to the cars was unclear and they subsequently lost interest. Who owned the unsold cars in the US – John DeLorean, the Bank of America, dealers who had paid a deposit and not received a car, or the receiver, as the last shipment of cars was despatched from Belfast without prior payment? The incident in Bridgewater a few weeks earlier hadn't helped matters.

My personal routine was almost back to normal. Each week I returned to the factory to assist in the procurement of materials to allow cars to be completed and shipped. My first stop once in Dunmurry was to talk to my friend Phyllis, now secretary to Brian Walker, the engineering manager. As employee number 21 she had been employed by the company from the beginning of the venture. Her first job was with the finance department, working for Brian Tanney for a year or so; then for Peter Allison, who ran the safety and emissions department; finally Brian Walker.

As I began to smarten up in the washroom before my grand entrance to her office, I realised how much my appearance had deteriorated over the previous three years. My image in the mirror was not one that

I recognised. Dark shadows under my eyes, with my size 14-inch neck poking through a size 16-inch shirt – those, together with my dishevelled appearance, would have earned me a part in a horror movie. From the start of the programme I had lost significant weight and now checked in at 126lb (9 stone). Even so, Phyllis liked me. Why I'll never know.

Supporting the manufacturing team to obtain parts for the build-out programme and travelling to Belfast to complete the task was part of my weekly cycle. As we ran short of materials to complete the cars we had two possibilities. The first was to obtain the material from the production supplier on a cash upfront basis as and when the supplier would assist. My job was to convince the suppliers, many of whom I knew well, that it was in their interest to keep the DeLorean programme alive. Procuring parts from suppliers was the easiest route if the supplier would co-operate. If not, and this occurred many times, the second possibility was scavenging parts from other vehicles already partly cannibalised.

The Middle East cars were an example of this activity. Parts for them were scavenged from earlier cannibalised vehicles, as assembly operators improvised to complete cars, obtaining parts from anywhere possible. The receiver didn't care about the accuracy of the specification or the pedigree of the parts on the car; his sole objective was to sell cars that were safe and of merchantable quality.

Initially there were 22 cars sold to Kuwait. Given the time and effort put in by the retained skilled workers, these were some of the best quality vehicles built, or more accurately completed, at Dunmurry during receivership. They were shipped on time and looked magnificent; we waited for the observations and plaudits from the distributor in Kuwait. When we received their comments we were devastated. All the cars could be opened with the same key. An engineer was sent to Kuwait on the next plane to rework the vehicles.

Each time I returned to DMCL there was usually another face missing from the ranks, axed by the receiver as unwanted baggage. These people had given their heart and soul to the company and many had placed DMCL as priority number one in their lives. They were dismissed by way of a photocopied letter with their name typed in a vacant space, no word of thanks, just legal jargon stating the receiver's obligations for payment of wages.

One by one the number of employees in Belfast shrank.

At first it was difficult to see who was in control of the Belfast operation. Don Lander had moved to the New York office. Myron had disappeared but would resurface in the US in early October 1982, three weeks before John DeLorean's arrest on drug charges, when he tried unsuccessfully to sue his former boss. He alleged that a scandal surrounded the financial demise of DMC and, because of his affiliation with John DeLorean, he had suffered damage to his reputation. George Broomfield left the company in April. Mike Loasby departed at the end of April. Shaun Harte stayed on for a while, undertaking sales and promotional work for cars to be sold outside the US. He left the company in October 1982.

On the UK domestic front, in early April Argentina invaded the British Overseas Territory of the Falkland

Islands in the South Atlantic. DeLorean were now not only off the front pages of the newspapers but were also not mentioned inside either. All news related to the Falklands War.

My first date with Phyllis was the third week of April; we met again later in the month. We had heard rumours from New York regarding potential investors or deals. At one stage there was an unnamed Arab state seemingly willing to invest millions in the DeLorean venture, and there were others, none of whom we or Sir Kenneth Cork believed had any credibility. We had grown to be sceptical about each new investor presented by John and eventually ignored any information that didn't originate from the receiver. The receiver's credibility increased as John DeLorean's waned. We heard about another investor, Peter Kalikow, a real estate agent. This one sounded real, but by mid-May that deal had also fallen through.

Sir Kenneth Cork did everything to keep the plant alive. He travelled to the United States on a regular basis to discuss various options and to discuss the latest saviour found by John. We thought that he would eventually triumph, otherwise he would have closed the plant in February 1982.

Other hungry mouths from Belfast were also after the Chancellor's purse. On 28 April the UK government announced that a further £47.6 million would be made available to Harland and Wolff in Belfast, bringing their support to a total of £206 million. (The company had traditionally employed workers mainly from the Protestant community.) James Prior commented that 'in return for this investment the company will take all steps to reduce its operating costs and improve efficiency ... so that the heavy burden on public funds can be progressively reduced'. We read the news, as did the workforce, and wondered if there was a different agenda for West Belfast and the DeLorean community than that offered to Protestant East Belfast. The Protestant community had a voice in Parliament by way of their association with Margaret Thatcher's Conservative party. The Catholic community were championed by a few politically non-aligned MPs, whose voice counted for very little.

In late April, two days after Mike Loasby's departure, Zora Arkus-Duntov wrote to John DeLorean offering to become chief engineer of DMCL and stating that he could fix the problems on the car. He said he knew what was required and was prepared to relocate to Northern Ireland for a period of two years. But it was not within John DeLorean's gift to appoint him. His letter and those that followed were ignored.

At weekends, mainly on Saturday mornings, Barrie Wills and I met at the Coventry office to review outstanding issues and catch up on the week's activities. One Saturday I was delighted to see Chuck Bennington in the office. Weeks later, following a number of Saturday mornings of the same ritual and of being pushed into the background, Barrie and Chuck confided in me their plans to take over the Dunmurry plant. The press would call them the 'UK consortium' group of businessmen.

I was keen to participate in any way that I could; I thought we had a real chance. However, my optimism diminished when, on 24 May, the receiver announced that as a buyer had not been found for the plant it would close the following week. Just 200 employees were to be retained to finish the remaining cars. I thought that this was certainly the end, but the final comment from Sir Kenneth was to the effect that the 'receivers will carefully consider any serious interest which might result in a viable future for the business'.

Following the announcement of redundancies the unions held a meeting outside the factory gates to discuss the way forward. Some workers climbed the gates and commenced a site sit-in which would last for eight weeks, with 256 employees joining in the protest. No management or salaried staff were allowed into the factory until the protest ended. Hand-painted banners on the DeLorean gates read 'We want work' and 'We demand our rights'.

As a result of this temporary eviction from the site, and much to the credit of the receiver, the remaining management team and support staff were given a temporary home two miles away at the ex-Olympia typewriter factory at Boucher Road in Belfast. Sixty DeLorean staff were relocated to the building, including employee number 21, Phyllis.

During this period the remaining senior management team met at Warren House to discuss day-to-day activities. This house, on the edge of the DeLorean site, was from May 1982 the residence of Barrie Wills, de facto managing director of DMCL. Shaun Harte was left to concentrate on the international sales activity covering Europe and the Middle East.

The Falklands War was now over, and on 8 June President Reagan arrived in Britain as part of a

European tour. He addressed the House of Commons that day, later holding private talks with Margaret Thatcher. On 24 June Mrs Thatcher visited President Reagan in Washington. The two became firm friends. This was a close bond.

By mid-June things were looking positive for the company. Sir Kenneth Cork issued a press release stating that he was 'very optimistic that the company could be back in production by the autumn, employing 1,000 people'. He continued: 'Two financial institutions were studying a takeover bid from an unidentified British consortium for the DeLorean plant.' I was a junior partner in this enterprise; to see this in the press was an incentive to continue the effort. We reviewed everything that would give us an edge, including discussions with Honda for the potential supply of their power train for the DeLorean, to replace the PRV unit.

The consortium was given until 30 August to submit a credible plan. If they failed by this deadline it would be the turn of John DeLorean; he agreed to the receiver's schedule, which was signed on 24 June. But, as usual, John DeLorean couldn't wait. That same day he issued his own press release, announcing to the world, as if to spoil our plans: 'Good news – we're on the way back.' He explained that Don Lander would be managing director of both the US and Belfast operations. In a private letter to a car dealer in the US he wrote: 'We've lost a number of people in the process (of downsizing) but those remaining are the best, gutsy, loyal, tough and believe in what we're doing.'

He also submitted his financial plan. Given John

DeLorean's history of financial planning, it's unlikely that the receiver gave any credence to the proposal. Sir Kenneth knew the only chance of salvaging the Dunmurry operation lay with the UK consortium.

I was asked to assist in the compilation of data for submission to the receiver. This included a cost and capital investment summary for the four-seater DMC24 and an identification of cost reductions on the DMC12 in the lower volumes we planned to make.

A board of directors for the new company was included in the submission, including a new president of the board. He was a well-known ex-managing director of a large UK vehicle producer. The line-up was impressive. The whole package was inspiring.

In late June Chuck invited me to lunch to meet a representative of a company well known in financial recovery programmes of the type that the consortium was planning. The discussion, as far as I am aware, went well. During the conversation I was asked if I knew of any improper financial transactions between Belfast and New York. (He was, of course, referring to the GPD affair.) I answered in the negative because all I had heard were rumours.

A week later Chuck asked if I would collect a drawing from Brighton, on England's south coast. The man I was to meet was a stylist for a well-known car design house in the area. Chuck had commissioned a sketch of a restyled TR7 for use in promotional work with the banks and the UK authorities. The last TR7 had rolled off the production line six months earlier. The sketch was used in the business plan as part of the submission to the government. The consortium planned to make a modified TR7 alongside the DMC12 in the Dunmurry factory, courtesy of the UK government, owners of British Leyland and the now redundant TR7 body dies.

The team worked long hours and at weekends to complete work on the recovery plan. When finished it not only looked financially viable but also imaginative, complete with a two-model line-up. This was something the receiver and the government applauded and had regarded as a fault in the original DeLorean deal back in 1978.

The consortium held meetings with British Leyland regarding the transfer of the TR7 body dies to Ireland. This involved the manufacture of TR7 body panels at August Lapple in Carlow, who had made the stainless steel pressings for the DMC12. A change of name was required for the new car as British Leyland wouldn't allow the TR brand name to be transferred. The name chosen for the revamped TR7 was to be Healey. Healey is a name of legend – the Healey 3000, Austin Healey and the Austin Healey Sprite. It was a brilliant marketing plan and seemed certain to succeed, or at least that's what we thought. Geoffrey Healey had agreed, under a royalty arrangement, to allow the name to be used for the revamped TR7/8.

A major problem to be resolved was the painting of the metal body panels for the modified TR7 as the Dunmurry facility didn't have painting facilities. One idea was to use the redundant facilities of Nissan in Dublin; their assembly plant had recently closed due to European Community competition guidelines on localised manufacture. The plan was to press the panels at August Lapple, ship them 50 miles to the ex-Nissan facility, and then move them onwards to Belfast for assembly at the Dunmurry factory.

The finished car would be a variation of the TR8 which enjoyed the benefit of the Rover V8 engine made available by British Leyland, or more precisely their owners, Her Majesty's government.

The Rover V8 engine has an interesting and relevant background to this story. In January 1964 Rover Cars Ltd gave their American head of operations, a certain J. Bruce McWilliams, permission to investigate the possible purchase of an American V8 engine for Rover. The all-aluminium engine was eventually made under licence by Rover from the Buick division of General Motors and later redesigned by Rover. This is the same Bruce McWilliams who took over from Dick Brown at DeLorean in March 1982.

The plan compiled by the consortium seemed perfect; all that was needed was financial backing. John DeLorean would remain as the sole distributor of the DMC12 in the US, as was his right under the original agreement with the government in 1978. For the new Healey, and for the DMC12 in other international markets, it was open house for the distribution rights.

By the end of July the occupation of the DMCL factory site was over and we could return to our home at Dunmurry. The receiver confirmed that he was willing to employ 200 workers to complete the remaining vehicles and to arrange the supply of spare parts to the US. The balance of 1,300 employees was made redundant; they were to be given their statutory allowance, which amounted to very little.

I was asked to assist in the final payout of the

employees. This took place in the canteen Portakabin. We were given a desk and a small container of letters addressed to each individual, arranged in alphabetical order. As an Englishman, and a member of the senior staff, it was with some trepidation that I entered the canteen that morning, but the men queued with dignity and the whole matter was completed in less than two hours, without any fuss or noise. Credit went once again to the Dunmurry workforce. I wondered why I had been so concerned.

As the UK consortium was on the final lap it was hoped that many of those who'd been made redundant would soon be able to return to work under the new management of the company.

The merchant bank Hill Samuel was the financier for the initial operation. Funding of the initial package to allow Hill Samuel to undertake the search for financial backers had been agreed. The receiver told the consortium that funding of the £80,000 needed for the first phase would not be a problem; various sympathetic bodies would take care of the cost. In a letter dated 23 July 1982 to Hill Samuel the consortium confirmed to the bank that all initial finances would be funded by the receiver and the Northern Ireland Office. They urged swift action as they wished to put matters in place to exhibit the cars at the International Motor Show in Birmingham, which was to open on 19 October. We now awaited approval from the government.

Life couldn't have looked better for me in late July 1982. Not only was it very likely that I would continue my employment with the company, in a job that would be the envy of anyone in the car business, but as a bonus my relationship with Phyllis continued to blossom.

However, John DeLorean's life was about to turn on its axis. He received a telephone call that would result in his financial ruin and disgrace, a call that would not only change the course of his life, but also mine and thousands of others, eventually resulting in the closure of the Dunmurry plant.

The caller was James Hoffman, a convicted drug dealer. He was a confidential informer employed by the FBI.

*Chapter 19*

# MARGARET THATCHER'S CHALLENGING YEAR

Margaret Thatcher didn't need John DeLorean's problems knocking on the door of number 10 Downing Street in early 1982. She had enough worries of her own. The year didn't start well for the Prime Minister and it continued its downward spiral through the early winter months of 1982. The misery seemed unrelenting as the problems at home and abroad continued to pile up in spring, and there was no improvement as summer arrived.

On 12 January she was told that her son Mark was lost in the Sahara Desert while taking part in the Paris to Dakar Rally. He'd last been seen on the Mali–Algerian border and the organisers had had no communication from him for the last two days. Three days later he was found alive. The assistance of a Hercules C130 search and rescue plane and other land-based search parties helped enormously.

On the UK domestic front, unemployment was increasing at an alarming rate. Unemployment in West Belfast was now twice the level it had been in 1978 at the start of the DeLorean venture. The recent redundancies at the factory were not helping the overall figures, although in March 1982 there were still 1,500 jobs remaining at the DeLorean site. Further gloom had come in early February when Laker Airways, a UK low-cost airline, collapsed with the loss of thousands of jobs and £250 million of debts. It was yet another problem and distraction for the Prime Minister.

On 2 April Argentina invaded and occupied the Falkland Islands in the South Atlantic, a British Overseas Territory. This resulted in the launch of the largest seaborne armada from Britain since the Second World War and would initiate the forging of a close and lasting friendship between Margaret Thatcher and Ronald Reagan, as described in the previous chapter.

There was now war for the United Kingdom on two fronts, fighting both the IRA, who continued their relentless bombing campaign in England and Northern Ireland, and the Argentinians some 7,500 miles away, who were mistakenly thinking that the UK would be too distracted by events closer to home to care about the tiny Falkland Islands that Argentina was now claiming as her own.

In early summer the Middle East conflict surfaced again, with the attempted assassination of the Israeli ambassador, Shlomo Argov, as he was leaving a diplomatic function at the Dorchester hotel in London.

On the industrial side, British Leyland was in a mess, suffering strikes and making constant requests for money and bail-outs. The vehicle maker was the biggest employer in the country, with 170,000 directly employed personnel and a further 400,000 dependent jobs at risk. Also looking for cash assistance were the nationalised company British Steel, and Harland and Wolff of Belfast, now a government-owned organisation too. These black holes, with their insatiable demands, were soaking up government money at an alarming rate, with no view as to when the continuing requests for financial support would end. The latest estimate in 1982 of financial assistance to the main recipients was £473 million to British Steel, £370 million to British Leyland and £139 million to British Shipbuilders (which now included Harland and Wolff), a total of £982 million in state aid.

Margaret Thatcher didn't need another lame duck in the guise of John DeLorean snapping at the heels of the government, causing distraction and adverse press coverage disproportionate to the scale of his tiny company in Belfast. The 1,500 remaining jobs at DeLorean was an insignificant total compared to the other chicks in the nest, and Northern Ireland was not seen as politically important as far as votes in the House of Commons went. There wasn't much sympathy in general for Northern Ireland at the time, and certainly none for John DeLorean.

Mrs Thatcher would have been informed by Sir Kenneth Cork just a few weeks after he took over as receiver that he had identified a hole in the original DeLorean equity funds that were the basis of the 1978 agreement. It seemed clear that a huge amount of investors' money had been misappropriated, either by John DeLorean or by others. How could the Prime Minister sanction resurrection of the company while John DeLorean was still involved? The simplest thing would be to allow the matter to disappear completely. But John DeLorean and others had not been investigated, charged or tried for any offence, and they probably wouldn't be for some time. The problem of the factory and the workforce, on the other hand, had to be resolved immediately.

The Prime Minister may have considered the words imputed to King Henry II of England in the 12th century, who was constantly at odds with Thomas a' Becket, the Archbishop of Canterbury. 'Will no one rid me of this turbulent priest?' the king is supposed to have said in anger. This was interpreted as a royal command and obeyed without question by sycophants at court.

The simplest solution to the DeLorean saga was to close the plant in Belfast, but a backlash from the Catholic community in West Belfast would be certain to fuel the fires of unrest, no doubt assisted by the IRA. The government continuing to pump money into the Protestant and clearly ailing Harland and Wolff, and making no attempt to save the jobs at DeLorean, would be seen as religious bias, with the Nationalist parties likely to suggest that Westminster didn't give a hoot about the Catholic community.

Actually there was no religious bias in Parliamentary circles regarding the Catholic community, but there was a significant dislike and mistrust of John DeLorean, given his recent history of negotiations with the government and suspected fraud. In the event, his arrest in October 1982 suited the government very nicely indeed and led to the plant's final closure.

When Thomas a' Becket was attacked on the steps of Canterbury Cathedral by the king's fanatical followers the assassins allegedly said, after striking their mortal blows, 'Let us away, knights; this fellow will arise no more.'

After his trial for drugs trafficking John DeLorean didn't rise again either; he was finished. In earlier times John was often quoted as saying 'Got some shit on his shoes' when referring to staff who had left his employment on less than amicable terms, a comment which might spoil their future job prospects while their former employer retained his credibility. John DeLorean certainly had an abundance of the stuff on his shoes that day in October 1982 when he was arrested in room 501 of the Sheraton La Reina hotel in Los Angeles, following his entrapment by James Hoffman in a drugs deal set up by the FBI.

## Chapter 20

# RECORDING THE DECEIT

It is unclear where and when John DeLorean first met James Hoffman. According to John's own account, as he recalls in his autobiography *DeLorean*, they first met in California in April 1978 when they chatted on DeLorean's drive in Pauma Valley after Hoffman had taken John's son Zachary to a motocross event with his own son, Tom.

It would be four years before John DeLorean and James Hoffman spoke again; the date of their next conversation was 29 June 1982, when Hoffman called DeLorean at his office in New York. That call was not recorded, and neither was the second call, but all future conversations, either by phone or in person, were tapped by the FBI.

John DeLorean wouldn't have known that Hoffman was a paid FBI and DEA (Drug Enforcement Agency) confidential informant. Initially he'd been employed to snare a suspected cocaine smuggler, Morgan Hetrick, but at some point – and again it is unclear when – Hoffman was offered John DeLorean as a celebrity prize by the FBI.

Back at the factory, by late July the UK consortium had finalised their business plan for restarting production at Dunmurry. Sir Kenneth Cork travelled to the US on 9 August 1982 to discuss arrangements regarding the distribution in America of cars made by the new owners, and the restricted role John DeLorean would play in any restructured US company; or, to put it plainly, for John DeLorean not to rock the boat and to keep quiet. Sir Kenneth also asked if DeLorean would relinquish his sole distribution rights for US sales of the car. John refused to discuss the matter.

The Cabinet meeting scheduled for mid-August was crucial to the success of the consortium's plan. James Prior intended to make his presentation to the Prime Minister; a stamp of approval from Mrs Thatcher was all that was required. Others in the Cabinet would follow her lead, as they always did. The lady in charge just had to nod as an endorsement to get the Belfast plant active and cars moving once again. As there was very little government money involved approval of the plan was judged to be a formality.

What occurred next is unclear. One record of the Cabinet meeting suggests that Margaret Thatcher thought that as the consortium was unable to raise the £80,000 from its own resources for the initial part of the activity to be undertaken by Hill Samuel, there would be doubt if it could raise the balance of the money required to restart production and introduce the TR7 derivative. In any event, she decided to veto the proposal.

Another account, as told by Sir Kenneth Cork to John Putt – leader of the DeLorean suppliers/creditors group, was that James Prior botched the presentation to the Cabinet and Mrs Thatcher threw out the plan. James Prior was not Margaret Thatcher's favourite minister and the conversation probably started on the back foot, with Prior knowing he would have a fight on his hands whatever he said, and on whatever subject he debated. But botching was actually not in James Prior's make-up.

There was nothing wrong with the consortium's proposal. Funding had been arranged and confirmed in a letter to the merchant bankers Hill Samuel in July. No government money was needed in the reconstructed company, except for the £80,000 that the NIO (Northern Ireland Office) and the receiver had agreed to finance, subject of course to the Prime Minister's approval. Which she now did not give.

Possibly the real reason for the proposal's rejection is that Margaret Thatcher knew of the GPD embezzlement but was not at liberty to share the secret with her Cabinet colleagues. By then she would have been informed that $17.65 million was missing from the DeLorean books, but knowing only that the money was missing with no details of who took it or its whereabouts. Through her contact with President Reagan in June/July she might also have known of the John DeLorean–James Hoffman drugs arrangement.

By a cruel chance of timing, only days before the crucial Cabinet meeting the UK satirical magazine *Private Eye* published yet another story about the affairs of John DeLorean and Roy Nesseth. The article, the second DeLorean revelation printed by the magazine during receivership, revealed further details of Roy Nesseth's criminal history and was scathing about his character. Nor was the article complimentary about John DeLorean. Details were given of Nesseth's threats of violence to Dick Brown and his family, and the long-term association between Nesseth and DeLorean was also described. By now Hill Samuel had developed cold feet and the whole package was beginning to crumble. It proved impossible to start over again.

Barrie and Chuck knew that their chance had gone. It was difficult to understand why it had been rejected, because the plan had credibility and would re-employ over a thousand of the workers who'd been made redundant earlier in the year. It had everything that Sir Kenneth Cork had asked to be included. Earlier concerns about the project, raised at the start of the DeLorean programme in 1978 by John Banham of McKinsey consultants, were answered. Hill Samuel had even prepared a press statement regarding their involvement, but after that Cabinet meeting the plan was dead in the water.

The agreement John DeLorean had signed with the receiver in June stated that after 30 August, if no other credible plan was in place to save the company, then it would be his turn to submit proposals to salvage the remains of the Dunmurry facility. Now the problem – and the slim chance of a solution – had landed in John's lap.

On Monday 30 August my home phone rang in the early hours of the morning. I thought that it couldn't be work as it was a national holiday in England, and anyway it was too early. But it was work; the call was from a colleague at the DMC facility in California. 'Hi, Nick,' he said, and went on to reveal that he had others with him, including directors of the company, who were working late Sunday night at the DeLorean facility at Irvine, California. They thought they'd call before I went to work that day.

'Can you arrange a consignment of parts for delivery to the US from the Dunmurry plant?' The voice then listed various service parts they required urgently. 'John is making plans for restarting production at Dunmurry and we need to support the dealers with the supply of service parts.'

I explained that the receiver was running the company and that I could not arrange any shipment without his blessing. This was conveniently ignored. 'We'll call back tomorrow our time and see what progress you have made.' He called my home number a few more times over the following weeks.

A few weeks after the first call from DMC in California I was warned that my phone conversations at home and at work might be tapped, as others believed their calls were being recorded. Was this due to the missing millions (the GPD affair) that we'd heard about earlier? I had nothing to worry about on this issue. True, we had spent almost £13 million of the government's kitty, but every penny had been accounted for in detail.

The tapping of UK residents' phone calls was initiated because of a telephone conversation that took place on 7 September 1982 between John DeLorean and James Benedict, an undercover FBI agent.

John DeLorean was under pressure to finalise the drugs deal set up by the FBI (posing as the supplying party). Under duress, John thought that he would counter the threats made to him and introduce what he considered to be his ace card. This was the involvement of the IRA in his dealings, acting as his banker for the drugs deal. But this was untrue.

He continued the falsehood by giving the name of a Northern Irish man he needed to contact in order to arrange the money for the drugs deal. The man John DeLorean mentioned had views that were the exact opposite to those of the Republican movement. So once again John had lied, but this new overseas connection would have to be investigated by the FBI.

Years later DeLorean acknowledged his deceit, saying that the FBI 'immediately checked out the supposed banker with British intelligence'. The IRA was not involved and the man he'd mentioned was the only name that had come to his mind when he was under pressure from the undercover FBI agent.

From the phone conversation on 7 September between DeLorean and James Benedict the FBI and DEA now had someone in the UK they thought was possibly assisting John DeLorean in the drugs deal. Were there any more names on John DeLorean's contact list in the UK? This was a new name to the FBI; they needed to monitor calls in the UK, but this was outside their jurisdiction. The UK authorities would assist for sure.

James Prior commented in the BBC documentary *Car Crash* that he was 'tipped off' regarding DeLorean's drug activities before the FBI arrested John in late October. The tip-off was likely to have been made in early September 1982. From this date, whatever happened with financing and recovery plans, DMCL was finished – at least as far as James Prior was concerned. It had probably been written off months earlier by Margaret Thatcher, who was likely to have known more details of the background.

Knowing the end game was near, James Prior asked Sir Kenneth Cork to wrap up the DeLorean business quickly and without fuss. On 1 October, not knowing that a storm was brewing on the other side of the Atlantic with the FBI and the sting operation, Sir Kenneth hurried John DeLorean for a credible plan. It's clear that the receiver was unaware of the events taking place behind the scenes in the US and the UK as he fought to save the factory, keeping all the doors and all the options open until the last moment.

In the US other battles were being fought, including, for President Reagan, one that was close to his heart: the war on drugs. On 2 October at 12.06pm the President made his weekly radio broadcast from Camp David:

'Now, regarding the other report I mentioned. In the next few days we'll announce the administration's new strategy for the prevention of drug abuse and drug trafficking. This is a bold, confident plan, and I'm elated. For too long the people in Washington took the attitude that the drug problem was so large nothing could be done about it... We've decided to do more than pay lip service to the problem... we beefed up the number of judges, prosecutors, and law enforcement people. We used military radar and intelligence to detect drug traffickers... but one thing is different now: we're going to be waiting for them. To paraphrase Joe Louis, they can run but they can't hide.

'We're undertaking a narcotics policy that might be termed "hot pursuit". We're not just going to let them go somewhere else; we're going to be on their tail.

'Now, you probably wonder why I'm so optimistic. Well, for the first time, the actions of the different government agencies and departments dealing with narcotics are being co-ordinated. There are nine departments and 33 agencies of government that have some responsibility in the drug area, but until now, the activities of these agencies were not being co-ordinated. Each was fighting its own separate battle against drugs. Now, for the very first time, the Federal government is waging a planned, concerted campaign... The mood toward drugs is changing in this country, and the momentum is with us. We're making no excuses for drugs – hard, soft, or otherwise. Drugs are bad, and we're going after them. As I've said before, we've taken down the surrender flag and run up the battle flag. And we're going to win the war on drugs.

'Till next week, thanks for listening, and God bless you.'

The President was speaking 17 days before John DeLorean's arrest. He repeated his comments at the Justice Department 12 days later.

On the John DeLorean front what came next was unexpected and would cause alarm within UK government, whose officials knew of events that were about to unfold. John DeLorean had managed to assemble a credible plan – not an unnamed Arab or other mythical investor but someone with integrity and money. The potential investor was Minet Management, a British company, and a member of Lloyds of London. They undertook high-risk, high-return investments and they had agreed to fund John DeLorean $100 million to restart his company.

This was not what the UK government wanted to

hear. The founder of DMCL was close to arrest, but his company was about to be saved. The government threw in one last obstacle. Any refunding would have to include a non-refundable personal investment by John DeLorean of $20 million. The deadline was set for 20 October. John DeLorean didn't have that kind of cash, and initially the figure of $20 million was regarded as impossible, but Minet Management could assist in bridging the gap via an association with a company that would lend DeLorean the money.

Step in FSI Management, headed by Jeanne Firman. She arrived at Dunmurry in early October, confirming a few days later that she would supply the additional money. All that was required now was for DeLorean to sign the paperwork and the deal was done, and then it would be back into production, building cars with John at the helm and the British government out of the picture altogether. John told Jeanne Firman that he didn't need the full $20 million – half of that amount would do and he would come up with the balance.

Sir Kenneth Cork arrived in Belfast on Monday 11 October and gathered the remnants of the management team together. Because they were unaware of recent developments it was thought that Sir Kenneth had chosen to appear in person to declare closure, like the decent man he was, rather than delegate the responsibility. Instead of the expected announcement, however, he asked that the company prepare for a new investor and make arrangements to re-employ up to a thousand ex-workers at the earliest opportunity. Ernie Benson from personnel recalls that the atmosphere was euphoric. They were told to wait a few days for John

DeLorean's deal to be finalised but that it was only a matter of time before we started production again.

It seemed that John DeLorean had done it again!

James Hoffman called DeLorean at his New York office on 19 October for confirmation that he would be on the west coast that afternoon to complete the drugs deal.

The deadline set by the British government for future financing and to have all the details in place was 20 October. The FSI loan paperwork arrived in the morning of 19 October and was placed on John DeLorean's desk in New York. It was to be signed by him and returned immediately to Jeanne Firman. John DeLorean's next step was the biggest mistake of his life. He chose to ignore the letter, instead travelling to Los Angeles to meet Hoffman and Benedict.

He was arrested at 3.15pm California time on Tuesday 19 October.

Cristina DeLorean arrived at Los Angeles airport just a few hours after her husband's arrest. Roy Nesseth was in tow but quickly shied from the cameras, preferring the shadows of the TV lights to hide his presence. But John's situation couldn't be sorted by big Roy's usual methods. The lads in this picture were bigger than him.

*Chapter 21*

# CLOSURE AND COLIN CHAPMAN'S LAST DAYS

O nly days after John DeLorean's arrest, and with astonishing speed, the IRS (Internal Revenue Service) in the US proudly announced that they had commenced investigations into John DeLorean's international financial affairs almost two years earlier in January 1981. The first letter referring to the activities of GPD landed on John DeLorean's desk a week before the first car was launched in Belfast. They had already invited DeLorean to submit details of the GPD contract to assess its tax liabilities. An audit by the Oppenheimer partnership was next; this was the financial group that was supposed to have invested in the Northern Ireland company, although not a single penny reached Belfast. In addition, US Federal officials said they had conducted a survey of John DeLorean's personal finances, which included a safe deposit box in a Caribbean bank.

Given the international nature of the GPD transactions – starting in Belfast, then moving to Geneva and finally to the USA – it's likely that the IRS contacted their associates in the Inland Revenue for advice at the start of their investigations, thus allowing the UK authorities an opportunity to conduct their own inquiry.

Prior to John DeLorean's arrest there were at least

three US agencies monitoring his activities: the Federal Bureau of Investigation, the Drug Enforcement Agency and the Inland Revenue Service. In the United Kingdom it is likely that the Inland Revenue was involved in DeLorean affairs and, according to John DeLorean in his autobiography *DeLorean*, the British Secret Service as well.

John DeLorean's hearing in Los Angeles initially set bail at $10 million; after an appeal it was reduced to $5 million. The *New York Times* recorded that a further reduction had been requested as John DeLorean required $130,000 per month for living expenses.

The *Chicago Tribune* wrote: 'When the judge in Los Angeles set his bail, his attorneys told the court that John DeLorean's living expenses totalled $130,000 a month. This included $33,000 a month for the farm, $10,000 for the New York co-op, and other fixed expenses. Plus a life insurance policy that cost $40,000 a month. None of these were particular extravagances. The farm is a $3.5-million, 430-acre estate in New Jersey. The New York co-op is a $5-million, 20-room Fifth Avenue duplex. The insurance policy is for $10 million. Extravagance is clearly in the eye of the beholder.'

For the remaining workforce in Belfast, many of whom were living off less than 1% of John's monthly allowance, it was clear this was the end of the company. The disgrace was not only John DeLorean's but also all those who had sold his dream down the line. We would be dismissed. There were to be no more reprieves. Most of the remaining staff received a letter terminating their employment with immediate effect.

Phyllis received her notice the following Friday; a few

days later she arrived in England to find a job near to the area where I lived. We had a wonderful two weeks, but this wasn't to last long because I'd been given a stay of execution by Barrie Wills and the receiver who asked me to work in Belfast until the end of the year. I'd be assisting Consolidated International in the transfer of material to their offices in the US and helping with the procurement and identification of parts. The company was about to finalise a deal with the receiver to buy the cars and parts remaining at the factory.

I locked the doors of the DeLorean Coventry office for the last time on Friday 5 November 1982. The remaining employees enjoyed a farewell drink at the local pub across the road, but I had to return there early the next day to collect 2,323 drawings, bills of materials and associated documentation for the DMC12 to keep safely stored in my garage at home. Just in case… just possibly… someone might need them.

Monday morning, 8 November, was an odd day. Just two weeks earlier Phyllis had travelled 350 miles by ferry and road to England, and now I was on my way to Belfast, to a location only a few hundred yards from where she had started out on her journey.

As the receiver wouldn't pay my hotel bills in Belfast I needed somewhere to rest my head – and for free. Barrie offered me space in the Warren House, in the main house. The caretaker's flat in the main building was now occupied by Barrie (former occupants were Chuck Bennington and Don Lander); the Warren House was one of five company houses purchased for the directors of DMCL, all later sold at auction. The gold taps that had caused so much bad press a year earlier were in the main bathroom of the

Warren House, although they were actually no different from those in my own bathroom at home.

Sir Kenneth had commenced a search for his own 'gold' in late summer 1982. To be precise, he was looking for the $17.65 million that had gone 'walkabout' at the start of the programme. His quest was to find the money; if it had been misappropriated then he needed to locate the cash, arrange for its return and prosecute the perpetrators. Although there had been rumours for almost a year regarding this missing money, details were known only to a few.

The receiver and his staff identified the hole in the finances at DMCL shortly after taking control of the company but had yet to identify the detail of the financial transactions involved in the embezzlement.

That was until the week of 8 November 1982, when a letter arrived from Jacques Wittmer representing the lawyers Helg, Grandjean, Picot, Sidler and Wittmer; the letter was postmarked Switzerland. The Swiss lawyers were the nominated escrow agents for $8,500,000 contracted between GPD and John DeLorean. Innocently, Jacques Wittmer wrote to the receiver in Belfast to ask for direction on how to dispose of the $396,000 remaining in the escrow account. The original contract stipulated that in the event of John DeLorean's incapacity the lawyers should contact DeLorean Motor Cars in Belfast to advise on disbursement. Which they now did. The cat was now out of the bag.

On the other side of the Atlantic and shortly after John DeLorean's arrest, Citibank asked the Dutch bank Pierson Heldring & Pierson to forward money held in another escrow account in John DeLorean's name to pay off the secured loan they had made to John in 1979. Due to John DeLorean's altered circumstances they wished to terminate the loan agreement. Citibank contacted the DMC trustees in the USA to make the necessary arrangements. The trail of the missing money started from there and could be worked back to the GPD agreement in Geneva in November 1978. The letter on the receiver's desk in Belfast completed the ring.

Sir Kenneth Cork now had more information to allow a meaningful discussion with Colin Chapman and Fred Bushell (group chief financial officer of Lotus). He met them in October 1982 at Lotus Cars. Colin Chapman had delayed this meeting for several months but eventually had no option but to accede to the receiver's wishes. Sir Kenneth questioned Colin Chapman and Fred Bushell about the GPD affair and requested details of the deal between Lotus and DeLorean. According to Sir Kenneth's account of the discussion, recorded in his book *Cork on Cork*, he didn't get very far. He said that the conversation was all 'up hill'.

On his return to Belfast Sir Kenneth located a copy of a GPD contract in the executive suite at Dunmurry and was keen to talk to Colin Chapman again, particularly as his copy of the GPD contract differed from the one held by Chapman. The two GPD contracts in question gave different addresses for GPD as well as listing differing terms.

A letter found in the executive suite at Dunmurry dated 1 November 1978 and written on Lotus Cars headed paper, signed by Colin Chapman and Fred Bushell, and addressed to the DeLorean Research Partnership and DeLorean Motor Cars Ltd, gave a guarantee of timely and full performance under the agreement with GPD. The chain was now complete, linking all three parties to the deal: John DeLorean, GPD and Lotus Cars.

Earlier annual accounts of Group Lotus had failed to declare the GPD contract in the Lotus books; Colin Chapman knew that withholding details of the income and profits of the deal from the shareholders was fraudulent. Given the knowledge the Inland Revenue now had regarding GPD he had no option but to declare the deal.

By late 1982 Group Lotus's empire had shrunk to 500 employees, with a total output of 600 cars for the year. American Express was demanding repayment of a £2.2 million loan and suppliers were snapping at the heels of the finance department. It seemed all their financial affairs were in crisis. The company had made a loss of £109,000 in 1981, the accounts were late, and the GPD name was mentioned for the first time in the company's submission to the tax authorities (although it is possible that the Inland Revenue had known about the GPD deal two years earlier from their counterparts in the US).

Colin Chapman was in deep trouble and risked arrest. Despite this, he had a busy week ahead from Monday 13 December. A second meeting with Sir Kenneth Cork would have to be postponed until later in the month as he couldn't cancel his two main appointments for that week. His first engagement was at the annual Anglo-American Chamber of Commerce celebration in London; the main speech was given by Henry Ford II. David Wickins joined Colin Chapman at the event. (Wickins was later to become chairman of Lotus, following Fred Bushell's resignation from the post.)

Two days later Colin Chapman travelled to Paris for

a meeting with FISA, the governing body of Formula 1 motor racing. He arrived on 15 December, flying from Hethel in his twin-jet Citation. Later that morning he met officials of FISA at their offices at Place de la Concorde in central Paris.

In the early evening he met his friend Jerry Juhan who, together with his wife, Marie-Denise Juhan Perrin, had brokered the GPD deal. Jerry Juhan had flown in from Geneva to meet Chapman. Although the reason for the meeting is unknown, it's likely that GPD was high on the agenda.

The return flight to Hethel took off from Paris at 9pm. The journey was uneventful and, according to Gérard Crombac in his book *Colin Chapman: The Man and his Cars*, Chapman sat in the co-pilot's seat for the latter part of the flight. The Citation aircraft was met at Hethel by two officials from HM Customs, a mandatory requirement for all flights originating from the continent. Also present were two trained Lotus security guards operating the control tower (guiding the aircraft to the ground), and the Lotus fire tender.

In the early hours of the next day, at his home at East Carleton, less than half a mile from Hethel, Colin Chapman suffered a massive heart attack and died. Tony Rudd and Mike Kimberley broke the news to the Lotus workforce later that morning. The autopsy recorded that Chapman died from acute heart failure caused by atherosclerosis, narrowing of the coronary arteries, a heart condition that builds up slowly over the years; untreated, the disease is fatal. So Sir Kenneth Cork never had his second meeting with Colin Chapman.

I heard the news of Chapman's death while driving in England, where I'd been collecting components from a supplier in Leicester. I'd been asked to collect the parts and deliver them to Belfast on behalf of Consolidated International, the company that had taken first option on the DeLorean facility, cars and parts. In an agreement dated 9 November 1982 between the receiver and Consolidated International the latter had agreed to purchase 1,041 completed DeLorean cars and another 77 in the process of assembly. Consolidated had also agreed to procure excess material at quantity and type to be nominated, at their discretion. They were granted first option of DMCL's assets as well, with a view to recommencing production at the Dunmurry site. This option would expire in 45 days.

Ironically, the cars shipped from Dunmurry to Consolidated were financed through ECGD, a financial service John DeLorean claimed he had been requesting from day one of the project but had never received. I assisted the finance people as we ploughed through the details of VIN (Vehicle Identification Number) records and checked each full VIN against each set of paperwork. Any error would cause the whole shipment to be held up pending correction.

On 10 November 1982 the High Court in Belfast agreed to a winding-up order for DeLorean Motor Cars Ltd submitted by Renault/COFACE; DMCL was now dead. I was told that I now worked for DSQ Property Services Ltd. My payslip reflected this, but it all seemed rather odd; the name didn't have quite the same appeal as its predecessor.

Cars for the Consolidated shipment were completed

with parts found by cannibalising vehicles or procuring components from ex-vendors; this was often a significant challenge as many were owed money for parts previously supplied. I was asked to accompany the Consolidated representative and to assist him in any way that he asked. This was a major task. The man was clearly uncomfortable working in Belfast; the locals couldn't take to him; possibly he felt threatened by the environment, and insecure. However, he lacked life's basic social graces and was direct to the point of being rude. The sooner I could get away from his company the better. The situation and atmosphere in the plant were bad enough without his charmless presence.

While in Belfast I'd often go to watch the action in the main assembly building, to see the last cars being completed. Entering this huge building with a floor area of six acres was perhaps the most depressing of all the activities I witnessed in receivership. What had once been a hive of activity, redolent with the noise of hydraulic tools, workers' voices and other sounds associated with car assembly, was now mostly silent and almost empty. The lights were switched off for the majority of the interior of the building, except for a small corner where cars were being completed. The area now in use was just a tiny fraction of the total space that had been utilised during peak production.

The main office area in the assembly building, once occupied by a hundred people or more, was now empty. Desks still housed the detritus of daily life, lying in wait for their owners to return – the remains of small snacks bunched up with papers spread over desk tops, files, rulers, biros. It was as if the residents had nipped out for lunch. It was a strange and unnatural scene; it felt eerie. Each time I passed the dimly lit manufacturing office I recalled, one by one, the name of each person who'd occupied a particular desk and imagined them on the phone or speaking to a colleague.

Each week that I returned to the assembly building the area where the cars were being finished had diminished, as had the number of people involved. Eventually, in December 1982, the last cars were completed in the training building. The company had turned full circle; it had come back to the training building where it had all begun.

There was a significant amount of camaraderie on the production line in the factory and with what was left of the management team. Some amusing moments helped to defuse the tension. In late November, towards seven o'clock in the evening, Barrie and I were looking out from his office on the first floor of the training building over to the factory buildings and pondering what might have been had the government accepted the UK consortium's package. The factory street lights that had once illuminated the way through the plant and floodlit the main buildings were now turned off. Only the outline of the factory buildings could be seen in the light of the full moon. Suddenly the phone rang and Barrie answered it. 'There is a man on the phone,' said a security guard, his voice full of excitement, 'and he says that he can save the plant and the workforce and can he speak to the man in charge.'

'Who's calling?' asked Barrie.

'Basil Wainwright,' said the security guard, after a few seconds.

Barrie said to me, 'It's your mate. Do you want to speak to him?' I knew instantly who he was talking about. This was the same man who'd offered the 'wonder product' plasma ignition to John DeLorean and years later claimed to the world that he had found a cure for AIDS. He was now a convicted felon (for other unassociated matters). Barrie and I collapsed in laughter. It took us a few minutes to regain our composure. I can't recall if I spoke to Basil Wainwright that night, but he certainly brought a smile to our faces.

Eventually the last shipment of material for Consolidated was ready. But the last box placed in the final container was different from the others. In it was a small cardboard coffin with an imitation body wrapped in a disposable paper overall (as used in the body shop), with a face cut-out of John DeLorean, taken from a magazine, tied around the hood of the overall. It was not intended to be disrespectful to John DeLorean, merely to register that this was the final scene of the DeLorean dream. The message was simple. This really was the end; the dream was now officially dead.

I left for home on 21 December, my fifth Christmas with the company. On 23 December Linda Shafran, representing Consolidated International, telexed the receiver to advise that they would not be exercising the option to recommence production at the factory. It was no surprise. Consolidated had got what they were after. There was never any intent to restart production, because manufacturing just wasn't in their blood.

I returned to the plant early in January and was told that my services were no longer required. I received the usual photocopy of the official notice of termination from the receiver. I took photographs of the few cars remaining in the training building; perhaps the last photographs taken at the DeLorean site. I left the factory for the final time on Friday afternoon, 7 January 1983, with mixed emotions of overpowering shame, disgrace, ridicule and immense pride.

My next visit to the factory would be almost 30 years later.

## Chapter 22

# SUNKEN TREASURE, TRIALS, FINES, FINANCES AND FIASCOS

The body press dies used by Lapple in Carlow for production of the stainless steel panels remained at their premises for some time after the DeLorean facility in Dunmurry closed its doors. All 33 tools, some weighing 20 tonnes or more, were stored safely at Lapple's factory in case they were required – and at one point during receivership this had looked very likely. Lapple held the tools as a lien against the debts owed by DMCL, but after the final whistle was blown by the receiver the Lapple plant manager, Helmut Jaeger, decided that they had outlived their use and the space was needed for other purposes.

The tools were moved to various scrapyards in Europe, including Spain, Portugal, Sheffield and Kent in the UK, and Cork in Ireland. At Haulbowline Industries' scrapyard outside Cork City, 12 large pieces of tooling were bought by Emerald Fisheries, who took them to Kilkieran Bay in County Galway. There, in an inlet off the Atlantic Ocean, they sunk the tooling to the bottom of the seabed, using them as anchors to hold fish cages in place for salmon farming. Photographs were taken by Captain O'Donnell, master of the *Severn Princess*, as the large dies were pushed overboard. One of the most complicated and expensive of the tools, the inner door press die, was ditched into Galway Bay in 1984.

Why did Captain O'Donnell take photographs when ditching the dies, which were just metal blocks that were of no importance to him and would now merely be used as harnesses to steady fish cages? Were the photographs taken as a souvenir or as evidence of ditching the tools beyond recovery? It's another mystery.

While this was happening John DeLorean was facing his own problems. His trial for alleged cocaine trafficking started at the Federal Court in Los Angeles in April 1984. US District Court Judge Robert Takasugi spelled out the law on entrapment: 'If you find John DeLorean committed the acts charged, but did so as a result of entrapment, you must find him not guilty.' Entrapment results if the idea for the crime stems from government agents or informants; if the defendant is induced to participate; and if the defendant was not predisposed to commit the crime in the first place.

One of the major flaws in the prosecution's case was the missing recordings of James Hoffman and John DeLorean's first and second conversations on 30 June 1982 and in early July. All other conversations were recorded. These two were the exception. It is difficult to believe that John DeLorean would initiate a drug-trafficking deal on the phone with a man he barely knew, in a manner similar to ordering a Chinese takeaway.

He was rightly cleared of all charges in August 1984, the jury convinced of the defence council's argument that John DeLorean was entrapped by the FBI. He might have been found not guilty of the crime, but his character was stained beyond repair.

The total investment by the UK taxpayer in the DeLorean venture was £77.46 million, with the addition of $12.6 million from the DeLorean Research Partnership (also known as the Oppenheimer group) and $5.15 million from the coffers of DMC/DMCL. Arthur Andersen, once a key player in the global accountancy business, had audited the DeLorean books but failed to notice the gap of $17.65 million left by the DeLorean–Chapman GPD deal.

The DeLorean accounts misrepresented or failed to disclose certain business transactions, namely those associated with money being deposited in the GPD deal. Sir Kenneth made stringent efforts to locate and recover the money that he said had gone 'walkabout'. The legal battles had begun – at first quietly, while Sir Kenneth collected the facts, and then in the courtroom. As with all things that had the DeLorean tag, matters took a few years to develop and were never straightforward.

The 15-count Federal indictment John DeLorean faced in September 1985 for the alleged GPD fraud focused on the $12.6 million the Oppenheimer group (DRLP) had invested for research into development of the DeLorean motor car and the ERM plastic process rights plus the $5.15 million missing from the DMCL accounts.

DRLP was formed in 1978 with 140 partners; Sammy Davis Jnr invested $500,000 and Johnny Carson lodged $100,000. The DRLP programme was facilitated by the New York investment broker Oppenheimer and Company; the objective of the investors was to achieve a tax shelter on any financial return occurring after DMCL commenced payment of royalties to the group.

The indictment in the fraud trial details the transfer

of $8.9 million to John DeLorean (equating to 50.1% of the GPD money). It was claimed John used this for a variety of purposes. The bulk, $7.5 million, was used to purchase the assets of Logan Manufacturing in Utah, a snow-grooming company; $0.875 million went to pay off a personal loan; the balance was for private use, including the purchase of jewellery from Citigold Inc. The remaining balance of the GPD money was transferred to other private accounts and never located.

GPD was a Panamanian company with its headquarters in Geneva; it had formerly been known as ILC (International Lotus Cars). Power of attorney for the company was with Marie-Denise Juhan Perrin in Geneva. Her husband Jerry Juhan had been involved in motor racing for many years and imported Lotus sports cars into mainland Europe. He was a close friend of Colin Chapman (and, as we saw in the last chapter, he had a meeting with Chapman just a few hours before his death).

The defence offered by John DeLorean's attorney was that the money transferred to John DeLorean's account was a loan from Colin Chapman – but as he had died two years earlier confirmation was not possible.

The jury found John DeLorean not guilty on all charges after what was described by some as a 'misdirection' by the judge to the jury. Alicia Nelson, a juror at the trial, wrote in detail about her experiences. She thought that the judge had directed the jurors voting for a guilty judgment to change their verdict to not guilty because a unanimous verdict was required in all Federal fraud cases. In fact, a mistrial was the option in these instances. Another juror, Ronald Nachtman, said: 'The way we interpreted the [judge's] instructions was that if we didn't agree he was guilty unanimously, he was to be acquitted.' Mark Sibula, another juror, said that he'd voted to acquit DeLorean, but three jurors who considered DeLorean guilty thought their only choice was to agree with the majority, as instructed by the judge.

DeLorean's ex-wife, now Cristina Thomopoulos, testified in a later bankruptcy trial and repeated the information at *Morganroth v. DeLorean* (regarding the debt to John's lawyer) that she had 'observed DeLorean practising forging signatures, ageing documents, handling documents with rubber gloves, and steaming open envelopes. She testified that she saw DeLorean practise the signatures of his business associates, Colin Chapman and Sir Kenneth Cork, and that on one occasion DeLorean gave her three documents that she knew were not authentic that bore forged signatures of Cork and Chapman. She testified that on one occasion DeLorean had her type up a phony transcript of a conversation that he had with Chapman.' (This comment was made in 1984.)

The 'not guilty' verdict was clearly a blessing for John DeLorean but the judgment led to another problem for him. He had stated during the trial that the $8.9 million transferred to his account by Colin Chapman was a loan – and loans by their definition need to be repaid. The court confirmed that the loan was owed to Chapman's estate but the response of the UK receiver, Sir Kenneth Cork, was, in effect: 'I'll take that, thank you very much, because Colin Chapman's estate owes it to us.'

John DeLorean eventually paid the receivers $9.5 million in 1992.

John's 'not guilty' verdict for fraud also gave the UK government a further headache. If they were to pursue Arthur Andersen, DeLorean's Belfast auditors, for $100 million and more for failing to identify the fraud allegedly committed in 1978 then John's innocence as decided by the court in New York suggested that he did not embezzle the GPD money. So who did? And was there ever a fraud?

Keen to sort out matters with the receiver, Lotus Cars Ltd agreed to pay £1 million in settlement while pleading innocent of any wrongdoing. This followed an £85 million tax bill being slapped on Lotus by the Inland Revenue as an incentive to ensure their full co-operation regarding the GPD affair. Given that Lotus Cars' net worth was probably less than £10 million at the time, the tax bill could be regarded as marginally on the excessive side.

Lotus received $137,167 of the GPD money and another £11 million for work on the car directly from DMCL. This was in addition to the money secretly paid to Colin Chapman.

In 1992 Fred Bushell pleaded guilty at Belfast High Court to conspiring to defraud, with others, DeLorean Motor Cars Ltd. He admitted to the embezzlement of $0.848 million. The Crown Prosecution Service stated that Colin Chapman took $7.542 million from the DeLorean equity money while a further $8.9 million went to John DeLorean. On 20 June 1992 Fred Bushell was sentenced to three years in jail, fined £1.5 million and ordered to pay costs of £100,000. Then a compensation order after a negotiated settlement added a further £2.94 million to Fred's bill. This included property, including Hethel Woods, adjacent to Lotus Cars at Potash Lane, once the home of Factory 6, the former USAAF intelligence headquarters at Hethel, and the DeLorean design office.

Fred was a friendly, personable man, extremely astute and knowledgeable about the automotive business. It was his brains that kept Lotus afloat during the lean years. On the odd occasion in the mid-1980s, when he was running the Formula 1 team, I would drop by Ketteringham Hall and I always found him civil and courteous. Once he gave me a tour of the building and its museum of Formula 1 racing cars. I was immensely impressed with him, the cars and the set-up at Ketteringham Hall. I would imagine John DeLorean came away with the same feeling after his first visit in August 1978.

In 1991 the receiver of the former DeLorean company, acting on behalf of the UK government, persuaded Colin Chapman's estate to part with £4.67 million, and the proceeds were shared between the Northern Ireland Office and the Inland Revenue.

In 1992, with some embarrassment, the Attorney General declared in Parliament that the UK government was unable to commence proceedings for John DeLorean's extradition from the US to stand trial for charges of fraud as the United States statute of limitations for the alleged crime had expired many years earlier. UK officials had had ten years in which to request his extradition but they had failed to register that the US legal timing of limitation was three years.

A legal battle in the Swiss courts with Jerry Juhan and his wife eventually resulted in an award of £180,000 to the receivers.

In an act of unbelievable spite the UK government sequestrated £990,000 from what they described as 'surplus' from the DeLorean Motor Cars Ltd pension fund for Belfast employees. It's still remembered with bitterness by ex-employees.

Following a settlement between the US DeLorean trustees and Arthur Andersen, Renault (COFACE) was paid $12.74 million. The payment was made to COFACE as they were the financing arm of the Renault deal.

Mixed news and complications followed for the UK government. A Northern Ireland Audit Office report of 2004 recorded this as follows: 'A civil hearing in New York in 1998 State Court found that Arthur Andersen had been negligent in failing to detect and report the fraudulent activities relating to the GPD transactions… adjudging Arthur Andersen to have been 60% to blame for the non-disclosure of the GPD fraud' (the corollary of this judgment being that DMC's officers and directors had been 40% culpable).

Why the DMC/DMCL companies didn't notice that the GPD money was missing remains a mystery. The money involved wasn't small change; it amounted to almost $18 million. There is no suggestion of impropriety, but in the three years the company was in business it failed to notice the hole in the finances created by the GPD affair. This task was left to Sir Kenneth Cork, who identified the gap in 1982 only a short time after taking over as receiver.

The UK government eventually settled their claim

with Arthur Andersen for £20.72 million. It's likely that the New Labour government, elected under the leadership of Tony Blair, demanded an end to the prolonged negotiations which were then in their 17th year. Before the agreement was reached the UK government had spent significantly more in the pursuance of monies than it had received in receipts. If the settlement with Arthur Andersen had not been agreed the UK authorities would have been considerably out of pocket, spending over £20 million in legal fees over those 17 years.

During the period that the various cases were in dispute the total legal fees for both sides (the UK government and Arthur Andersen) probably exceeded £45 million. That is more than half of the original DeLorean investment money used in building the car and the plant.

The total number of people employed in handling the legal actions was probably fewer than a hundred individuals over the period. There would have been no one from Twinbrook or Dunmurry on that list.

## Chapter 23

# AFTER CLOSURE

Within two weeks of leaving DMCL I joined Jaguar Cars at Browns Lane in Coventry as purchasing manager for the engineering division. Jaguar had incurred losses of £82 million over the previous three years yet was awarded £80 million in 1981 for development of their new car, the XJ40. Later the sum for capital investment increased to £200 million of government and UK taxpayers' money.

Although my colleagues were pleasant and professional people, and many were very talented, Jaguar was then a failing company that didn't have the will to live. Industrial relations were a nightmare and doing anything quickly was not a phrase used too often at Browns Lane. I had been hardened by the constant pressure to perform at DeLorean and it was likely that any job from now on would appear leisurely and pedestrian.

Although I admired the Jaguar product and the corporate history I didn't stay with the company for long. After a few years at Browns Lane I joined Lotus Cars as supplies director. There I enjoyed seven years of absolute bliss. Colin Chapman died three years before I joined, but his legacy remained in the daily life of Lotus. I regularly heard phrases he used, retold to all newcomers: 'Those who can, do, and those who can't, talk about it'. Another remark he used, maybe to compensate for some earlier unreasonable pressure was, 'Only the trees with fruit get picked'. Colin Chapman had both the carrot and the stick in his tool bag. During this period John DeLorean's trials came and went. I had little interest in his troubles, not even really feeling curious about his tribulations, his successes or failures. Later, however, I began to take an interest and began my research into all the details.

The facts have now been known for many years – that John DeLorean was entrapped in the drugs deal – but a question remains as to who initiated the process.

Was the plan to trap John DeLorean hatched in early June 1982 when Margaret Thatcher and her staff met President Reagan and his team in London, three weeks before John DeLorean received his first call from James Hoffman on 29 June 1982? Was the Prime Minister's wish to rid the UK of her 'turbulent priest' voiced to Ronald Reagan and his staff, and was John DeLorean's arrest used as a bonus to kick-start the President's high-profile anti-drugs campaign which began in October 1982?

The comments of Sir Keith Joseph, the UK Industry Secretary, made on 6 February 1981 tell one possible story. He wrote: 'The longer term future of the [DeLorean] project remains uncertain but if it is to fail, the committee agrees with the Secretary of State that this must be seen to be the responsibility of Mr DeLorean and not the fault of the [UK] government.'

The remarks of Gerald Scotti, a DEA agent involved in the entrapment of John DeLorean, also lend force to the theory of US government involvement in the entrapment. At John DeLorean's trial he said: 'I knew

from a long way back the [US] government would go
to any lengths to prosecute Mr DeLorean...'

Perhaps John DeLorean was entrapped by James
Hoffman of his own volition, keen to impress his new
employers, the FBI?

Judgment is with the reader. Certainly the nature of
John DeLorean's downfall provided interested parties
with a convenient exit from the Northern Ireland stage
and caused the reaction from employees, dealers and
suppliers that was intended. It also deflected criticism
that the government was selective in supporting other
ailing concerns, both domestically in Northern Ireland
and nationally in Britain, without being accused of
religious or industrial bias. In that respect it was a
magnificent job undertaken intentionally, or as a
consequence, by the initiators of the entrapment process.

Many things have been written about John
DeLorean. The best description I have read is that John
DeLorean 'was caught in the act of being himself'. His
insatiable appetite for success and money that resulted
in his lofty position on the 14th floor at General Motors
was the same trait that led to his demise.

The losers in this saga, however, were not John
DeLorean, who was declared bankrupt in 1999, or the
management team, many of whom found other jobs. It
was the 2,500 employees at Dunmurry. Many of them
never worked again.

Praise to the workforce of DMCL whose response
during the difficult times of the DeLorean programme
was magnificent and legendary. The outstanding effort
by many people and organisations including Lotus Cars,
the DMCL supply base, the workforce at Dunmurry and

Coventry, gave momentum to an effort to achieve what most people thought was an impossible dream.

If you drive down the Lisburn Road in Dunmurry today, past the Conway hotel, now a housing estate, you'll see the former DMCL site on the Creighton Road. The road was built after the company's collapse, but it had been planned in 1979 in order to take the burden of heavy traffic to and from the DeLorean factory. Mature trees on the perimeter of the former DMCL plant hide the site's industrial heritage. The high wire fence that surrounds the test track is still there after 30 years, a rusting monument and reminder of what could have been if we had done things differently and if only the senior executives had faced up to John DeLorean, restricting his dreams, restraining his activities, at least for a while.

Excessive overheads at Dunmurry, the consequence of overmanning of non-productive staff, contributed to the losses, but even this burden was dwarfed by the huge $800,000 a month operating cost of the US operations, mostly funded by DMCL in Belfast. Sooner rather than later these overheads would sentence the Dunmurry site to death. The ramp-up in production merely hastened the demise of the company.

John DeLorean's instruction to increase production in mid-1981 to satisfy the requirements for his public stock offering was the key decision that resulted in the early failure of the company. If he'd been patient and restructured the company to reduce costs the business would have survived for a few more years. A successful company would have hidden the GPD issue, which would have remained buried or, if uncovered, probably ignored. Undoubtedly some time later the DeLorean plant at Dunmurry would have been sold, with John DeLorean moving on to new pastures.

As a young man in 1978, coming to Belfast from England, many things were new to me, particularly the constant stream of bad news. Each day brought another death or injury through violence. The bloodshed I had witnessed on television in England before joining the company had seemed unreal and remote; turning off the TV solved the problem. Things were now different because the violence was real and tangible; it would not go away. Anguish became a way of life not only within the community but also in the factory, where we wondered from day to day what would be the next problem that would have to be resolved.

Thomas Niedermayer's death haunted me for many years. Ingeborg, Thomas's widow, never recovered from the depression she suffered following the discovery of her husband's body in 1980. She ended her life in 1990. After checking into a hotel in Bray, near Dublin, she walked into the sea fully clothed; her body was found ten days later 20 miles down the coast at Greystones. Gabrielle, her elder daughter, committed suicide in 1994 and Renate, the younger girl, a few years later. 'The Troubles' had claimed three more lives.

The Niedermayer family lost more than a fanciful dream or injury to feelings. Their loss was total.

Northern Ireland's other miracle is one of epic proportions. The peace process has transformed the country from a strife-torn, battle-weary forgotten land to one bustling with fresh confidence. The burnt-out buildings have long been replaced by impressive modern structures, and the high streets of the larger towns boast the names of the multinational companies that were afraid to invest in Northern Ireland 20 years earlier. Sectarian conflict remains in Northern Ireland but on a significantly lower level than was witnessed in the 1970s and '80s when the DeLorean dream arrived in Dunmurry.

The dream that took shape in Belfast has long disappeared, but the scars left by its operation and closure remain in many aspects of life in Northern Ireland today. The financial lessons have been learned. Debates in Parliament continue to offer the DeLorean programme as an example of malpractice and waste, the emphasis always placed on its negative aspects. There are very few tributes to Belfast's little miracle at Dunmurry and to the people who produced a car and a factory in 22 months, often in impossible circumstances. This story is one contribution to the positive elements of the DeLorean dream.

The brave politicians and civil servants who approved the DeLorean venture in 1978 gave the people of Belfast an opportunity to work and contribute to society. John DeLorean also gave them that chance; then took it away.

He was never convicted of any criminal offence.

He died on 19 March 2005.

# ACKNOWLEDGEMENTS

My invite to Ken Koncelik's superbly organised 2008 DeLorean Car Show in Gettysburg rekindled my interest in the DeLorean car and history of the company; this followed 26 years of shunning the name DeLorean in any form. The idea of the book started from that time.

Many people have assisted in my research, supplying data and encouragement on the numerous occasions I had abandoned the project.

James Espey of DeLorean Motor Cars in Texas gave encouragement and supplied hundreds of documents, many essential in completing a particular sub-story. Also Matt Sommer who gave equal encouragement and constant moral boosting emails, he also supplied many documents and photographs, as did Tony Swann and Rich Weissensel.

Robert Lamrock's collection of DeLorean-related material is unique. Robert supplied copies of many key documents for my story, his impressive array of contacts in the Belfast area allows him to produce the remarkable Eurofest Car show. Thanks to him the DeLorean dream lives on in Northern Ireland.

Sean Lynch has undertaken significant research in determining the fate of the DeLorean body press dies. I thank him for the information he has supplied, either directly or via his website.

Many Lotus employees from the DeLorean era retold their stories; thanks to Paul Fricker and Mick Weir, whose memory of their part in the project is quite astonishing. Former DeLorean employees supplied so much information that many of their stories have not made it into the book.

But key events are recorded. I spent many hours talking to Dixon Hollinshead, the man responsible for building the DeLorean factory; his recollections of the period remain sharp. I agreed only to record events that were of interest to the book. His wife Barbara (BJ) also supplied fascinating stories.

Thanks to Neal Barclay, an ex-employee of DMCL, who recounts the best job he ever had, and Harry Steadman, a senior manager on site at Dunmurry, for confirming that the bizarre events that occurred during the building of the factory and car were not imaginary. The stories related by Stuart Craven's and Ernie Benson on the gold cars and human issues front have been essential in completing my story.

Bob Dance, once Colin Chapman's chief mechanic, supplied details of the history of the Lotus site and Ketteringham Hall, invaluable when retelling the story of Hethel Airfield in World War Two. As was Fred Squires' account of the time (he rebuilt the 389th Heavy Bomb Group Chapel at Hethel).

Thanks to Matthew Harte, son of Shaun Harte, a senior director of DMCL, for supplying many documents not previously in the public gaze.

Finally to all those working for me in Coventry from 1978 to 1982, including Paul McVeigh, Roger Jarman, Jill Rooney, David Williams, John Bowerman, Stuart Craven, Gary Grove, John Sharp, Tony Mayo, Len Weaver, Geoff Gale, Hazel Higgins, Bernard Ferguson, Jayne Heather, John O'Rourke and Anita, all of whom were dedicated to making the project work and gave unquestionable loyalty to the DeLorean dream. And finally to Barrie Wills, my boss at DeLorean, whose resolve to continue whilst many would have conceded defeat was inspirational to many of us.

# BIBLIOGRAPHY

Ken Bloomfield, *Stormont in Crisis*, published by Blackstaff Press.
ISBN 0856405256

Peter Bodle and Paul Wilson, *The 389th Bomb Group in Norfolk*, published
by Liberator Publishing. ISBN 0955191610

Martin Bowman, *Airfield Focus*, published by GMS Enterprises.
ISBN 1870384989

Kenneth Cork, *Cork on Cork*, published by Macmillan.
ISBN 0333444795

Gerard Crombac, *Colin Chapman – The Man and his Cars*, published by
PSL. ISBN 0850597331

A.J. Davidson, *Kidnapped*, published by Gill & MacMillan.
ISBN 9780717135721

John DeLorean, *DeLorean*, published by Zondervan Books.
ISBN 0310379407

Ivan Fallon and James Srodes, *Dream Maker*, published by G.P Putnam's
Sons. ISBN 0399128212

William Haddad, *Hard Driving*, published by W.H. Allen.
ISBN 0491037732

Lee Iacocca, *Iacocca*, published by Bantam Books.
ISBN 0553251473

Brian Keenan, *An Evil Cradling*, published by Vintage.
ISBN 009999030X

Mike Lawrence, *Colin Chapman Wayward Genius*, published by Breedon
Books. ISBN 1859832784

Hillel Levin, *Grand Delusions*, published by Viking Press.
ISBN 067026685X

Michael S. Lief, H. Mitchell Caldwell and Ben Bycel, *Greatest Closing
Arguments in Modern Law*, published by Touchstone Books.
ISBN 0684859483

John Moore, *Motor Makers in Ireland*, published by Lagan Books.
ISBN 0865402648

Jim Prior, *A Balance of Power*, published by Hamish Hamilton.
ISBN 024111957X

Tony Rudd, *It Was Fun!*, published by Patrick Stephens Ltd.
ISBN 18522604131

Jane Beck Sansalone, *White Flak*, published by Regina Publishing.
ISBN 0966872207

Starr Smith, *Jimmy Stewart Bomber Pilot*, published by Zenith Press.
ISBN 10-0–7603-2199-7

*The DeLorean Tapes*, published by Collins.
ISBN 0-00217428–6

NIAO report, *DeLorean: The Recovery of Public Funds*, reference HC287,
published 12 February 2004.

# INDEX

BIBLIOGRAPHY